Solving Horse and Pony Problems

Solving Horse and Pony Problems

How to Keep Your Steed Healthy and Get the Most from Your Mount

Karen Bush and Sarah Viccars

with illustrations by Christine Bousfield

The Lyons Press

Guilford, Connecticut
An imprint of The Globe Pequot Press

The Lyons Press is an imprint of The Globe Pequot Press

10 9 8 7 6 5 4 3 2 1

Printed in the United States of America

Library of Congress Cataloging-in-Publication Data

Bush, Karen.
  Solving horse and pony problems : how to keep your steed healthy and
get the most from your mount / Karen Bush and Sarah Viccars ; with
illustrations by Christine Bousfield.
      p. cm.
  ISBN 1-58574-849-8 (pb : alk. paper)
  1. Horses–Miscellanea. 2. Horses–Health–Miscellanea. 3.
Horsemanship–Miscellanea. I. Viccars, Sarah. II. Title.
  SF285.B977 2003
  636.1'0893–dc21
                      2003011227

For the real
Stephanie Birchall
with love

Contents

Introduction

Horse or pony keeping is not always the bed of roses imagined; animals can hardly ever be relied upon to behave predictably, or even in the manner described in so many horse books.

Horse keeping, therefore, is seldom as straightforward as it at first seems, whether for the new owner, or for one who is more knowledgeable. This book does not pretend to solve all the problems that may possibly occur, nor does it claim to have found all of the solutions to those mentioned. However, it does try to highlight the common practical problems that people encounter, often overlooked by many books, and to give sound advice on coping and dealing with them.

It should also be of interest to those who have not yet acquired a horse or pony, as plenty of information of interest to the casual, or "weekend" rider, has also been included.

To Buy or Not to Buy?

Q. I am considering leasing a pony; I know both the owner and pony quite well, but nevertheless, are there any precautions I should take?

A. Leasing a pony can be a mutually agreeable arrangement for both the owner and the lessee; it may be up for lease for a number of reasons, ranging from the owner having outgrown it, but not wishing to part with it entirely, or due to lack of time or finances. However, there can be a number of catches for the unwary. A suitable horse or pony for lease may be heard of by word of mouth, or through advertisements in the "Pets and Livestock" columns of local newspapers, or in the "For Lease" sections of most horse magazines. Having found an animal that sounds suitable, both parties would then be well advised to proceed with caution.

From the lessee's point of view, the same priorities must be taken into account as when actually considering purchase. The initial outlay of buying may have been avoided, but thereafter the horse or pony will still need feeding, shoeing, regular veterinary attention, possibly stabling, and everyday care, which can still be a considerable financial drain. Suitable facilities must also be available where the animal can be kept, especially as the owner will probably wish to see the place in order to set his mind at rest before finally agreeing to a lease. The pony should be ridden by the prospective lessee when going to see it.

The owner will also want to know something about the lessee's capability and general level of knowledge about caring for a horse or pony properly, and is likely to ask a few questions about the sort of routine and exercise it is likely to receive, plus the activities for which it will be used. In return, the lessee must not only answer these questions honestly but inquire himself as to the age and veterinary history of the animal, and any conditions which may be attached, such as restrictions of use, and whether regular visits by the owner, with the opportunity of an occasional ride, are expected. Before agreeing to a more final and binding contract, the animal should also be checked by a veterinary surgeon for any physical defects that might prove to be a problem in the future. Which party pays for this service will have to be agreed upon; it is usually assumed that the lessee will, but the owner may agree to meet some of the costs. Should the results of the vetting prove satisfactory, then a contract between both parties should be drawn up by a lawyer. This should include the following points, which will require some discussion to reach a fair agreement:

Shoeing: It must be decided how frequently this will be done, and who will be responsible for the bills (normally the lessee).

Veterinary bills: The lessee is normally responsible for all of these, although the owner may agree to pay part or all of the bills incurred for annual vaccinations.

Insurance: The horse or pony should be insured (and the tack as well); the parties may agree to split the amount since this is also in the owner's interest, or the lessee may have to agree to pay all of it.

Saddlery: A list should be made of all items of saddlery, horse clothing, grooming tools, and so forth, which will accompany the animal. In the event of anything becoming lost or broken, the lessee is normally held responsible for replacement or repair. Tack should be carefully examined beforehand, since if it is very old and worn it will not only prove unsafe to use, but may cost the lessee a considerable amount.

Feed bills and rent: These are entirely the lessee's responsibility. The location where the horse or pony is to be kept should be stated, and the owner kept informed as to any changes.

Use of horse/pony: The activities it is allowed to be used for should be listed, since the owner may be anxious that it not take part in events where it is more likely to injure itself, such as hunting, or cross-country competitions. A mention could also be made here as to whether any other people, other than the lessee, are to be allowed to ride it.

Length of loan: Initially this is best kept to a fairly short period, if possible, say two to three months; if the loan is working out satisfactorily, it could be renewed for a longer period, after which the contract could again be renewed, reviewed, or terminated if desired.

Terms of notice for return: To be fair to both parties, this should also be agreed upon, so that the owner does not suddenly find a horse or pony returned, with no opportunity of organizing somewhere to keep it, or alternatively, so that the lessee does not suddenly find it whisked away having perhaps already made plans for future activities. A period of about a month is usually satisfactory. Provision should also be made for the return of the animal should it become incurably lame, or affected in some way that makes it impossible for the lessee to ride it again. Two copies of the contract, both signed by the owner and by the lessee, should be made, and a copy kept by each. It may seem overcautious going to such lengths, but even good friends have been known to have a falling out over less!

Q. My daughter has been riding for several years now, and helps out at the local riding stables every weekend, and several evenings during the week as well. Since she is so enthusiastic, and it is obviously not just a passing phase, I would like to buy her a pony. Where is the best place to buy from, and what breed would be best?

A. Auctions should most definitely be avoided, as it is impossible for the inexperienced to pick out something suitable—even the experts have been known to make mistakes! You could try a reputable local dealer, but you should sound out a few opinions in your area first. Most dealers are not the con men they are frequently portrayed to be, and cannot afford to risk their reputation, but they are nevertheless in business to make money, and some are perhaps a little less scrupulous than they should be. Your daughter is also far less likely to get such a good opportunity to really try out a suitable pony. Your best bet is probably to look through the ads in your local newspapers, and in the "For Sale" columns of horse magazines.

You could also inquire at the riding school where she helps out, as they may well have heard of something which would be right for her. You should enlist their advice and assistance if available. Having found one or two "possibles," ask an instructor who is familiar with your daughter's riding capabilities to come and have a look with you both. You will probably need to pay him or her for their time, but it can be very helpful in trying to make a sensible choice. When looking around for a pony, stick to the local area if possible, since you will be able to find out more easily about its reputation, and whether it really is the genuine animal that it seemed when you saw it. As far as breed is concerned, unless your daughter has specifically set her heart on showing, it is relatively inconsequential. It is more important that the pony is of the right size, build, and temperament for her to be comfortable with and able to handle confidently, and capable of performing adequately at whatever activities she will want to try her hand at.

Q. I realize that keeping a horse is likely to prove expensive—but what sort of bills am I going to have to consider if I do go ahead and purchase one?

A.　There are plenty of hidden expenses to consider when buying a horse or pony. First, you will need to pay for its accommodation; of course, it makes sense to have leased or otherwise secured the right to keep a horse in advance of acquiring the animal. On top of this, in the winter you will need to pay for hay, and if stabling the animal for all or part of the time, for bedding as well. There will also be bills for feed; you can work out how much these will roughly cost, plus the price of bedding, if you ask for a price list from your local feed dealer. You may need to buy new saddlery, and throughout the year it will need to be kept clean and repaired.

　　Even if no accidents occur, the vet will need to make two yearly visits, for teeth floating and to administer annual vaccinations. If an insurance policy is taken out, you should find it possible to insure against veterinary bills over certain amounts, which will help you out in a crisis. All the equipment necessary to care for your horse properly will need to be bought, including grooming tools, blankets, stable equipment, and mucking-out tools. On top of all this, any horse or pony you buy will need to be wormed every six to eight weeks, shod every four to six weeks, and you may find that you are also liable for a certain amount of stable and field maintenance. Financial considerations aside, you will also need to find plenty of time to look after it.

Q. Having found a suitable pony, should I get someone to look it over before buying it? It looks all right to me.

A. Ask your local horse vet to come and vet the pony at a time convenient for the owners. If possible, be present yourself so that you can see all that goes on, and so the vet can explain any peculiarities and the effect they are likely to have. "Vetting" consists of a really thorough examination, during which the animal is examined physically for any problems, ranging from defective eyesight, to unusual lumps and bumps, and a sound heart. A description is also written at this time.

The pony will then be trotted so the vet can check that he does not appear to be lame, and finally will need to be galloped and cantered in tight circles so that he can test the pony's wind. You will also be asked for what purposes you intend to use him, and the vet will finally produce a certificate, all being well, stating that he is sound for the purposes you want to use him for. Should the pony fail, do not disregard the vet's opinion, thinking that you know best, however disappointed you may be. Should something

Fig. 1. Horse being trotted for a vet.

go wrong after purchase in such a case, you will not be able to return the animal, and may be faced with hefty veterinary bills.

Q. I am considering buying my first horse—what sort of things should I take into consideration?

A. Make a list of your priorities so that you have a clear idea of what you are looking for—there is no point in wasting either your own (or other people's) time. Don't be too inflexible either, or your search for perfection could last you a lifetime. First of all, consider your finances; this will limit the amount you are able to spend, and reduce the number of ads that you have to look through. Money must also be considered when deciding what type of horse you want; an animal capable of living outdoors all year-round will obviously be cheaper to keep than one that needs stabling. It will also be less demanding on your time (although it will still need checking each day), and will be able to exercise itself should you be unable to ride for some reason.

Something fairly tough, preferably a breed noted for its hardiness, and already used to living out, would be most suitable in this instance, unless you have both the time and the money for an animal which is more finely bred and requires coddling. Decide on the height you would be comfortable with, and the build necessary. A 15 hh horse may be the right height for you, but may not necessarily be of a sturdy enough build to cope with your weight comfortably if you are fairly solid. In such cases, if you want to stick with that height, you will need to look around for something quite sturdily built. On the other hand, if you are of a slender build, something of the same height, but rather narrower and less strong will be more suitable if you are to remain in control. Unless you have any really strong dislikes, color or gender should not play a part in your choice; however, temperament and ability should. You do need to be totally honest with yourself about your capabilities, and stick to something which you know you will be safe on, unless you are a very confident and able rider ready for something more advanced.

If the animal is to become a companion with whom you will wish to spend some time, then a nice nature is also important. One that bites and kicks all the time is not very pleasant to handle, although these vices might be overlooked in a horse bought purely for its ability in competition. Consider also the activities for which you will want to use it; a good local riding club horse or Pony Club pony must have reasonably good conformation if it is to be at all successful and remain sound. Inferior conformation can be tolerated to a degree if the animal will not be expected to exert itself much more than for a quiet ride around the block.

However, do avoid buying an animal that suffers from a serious defect, or a minor one which is likely to become progressively worse. When trying out any horse or pony, give it a fair trial—ask if you can saddle it yourself, and having seen it ridden, put it thoroughly through all of its paces on both reins, and possibly take it over a small jump too. Should you feel that this is just the animal for you, make an appointment to see it once again the following day, or a few days later, so that you do not make a hurried decision in the heat of the moment. Consider it all carefully, and do not allow yourself to be pushed into anything, or you may regret it later.

Q. I am considering buying my first horse; should I ask for a bill of sale and, if so, what should be included?

A. Someone who is selling a horse or pony does not have to agree to sign a bill of sale. But it does have advantages. Providing it is reasonable in its specifications, and is fair to both parties and pro-

Fig. 2. A horse with a good conformation.

tects them, then at least both seller and purchaser know what each expects of the other as a result of the transaction. If a seller refuses to be bound by a contract, then it should certainly raise a few suspicions in the mind of the purchaser, and great care should be taken.

The names of both seller and purchaser, with their addresses, should be included in the contract, together with the agreed sum for the animal, which should be named and briefly described. The activities for which the horse is warranted sound should be stated, plus any exceptions, vices, or unsoundness. A length of time (usually not exceeding seven days) should be stated for the return of the horse if it is found not to comply with the description; and saying that it should be accompanied by a signed certificate from a qualified veterinarian specifying in what respect(s) the horse fails to comply. In the event of a dispute, a vet is to be agreed upon by both parties, whose decision is binding. Two copies of the contract should be made, dated, and signed by both seller and purchaser, and a copy kept by each. A lawyer can help with the wording; but it is inadvisable to sign any contract unless the animal has been vetted first.

2

Equitation—Flatwork

Q. I've been riding for some time now, but I still get saddle-sore. Is this because I'm not sitting properly? Or could it be due to the saddle?

A. There are several possibilities here, one of which could be that the saddle is very hard—riding-school saddles are not always known for their comfort, for example. Neither are older rigid-tree saddles as luxurious as spring-tree ones; if you want to know which it is, a spring-tree saddle will be stamped to that effect on the panel, beneath the flap. The problem could also be partly due to your build—if you are thin, you might try using a seat-saver made of sheepskin or synthetic fleece to provide a little more padding for the nether regions. These are also pleasantly warm during the winter months—and, if you do not wish to go to the expense of buying one, can easily be made yourself from remnants. The way in which you are sitting is another possibility; if you tip forward and perch in the saddle rather than sitting squarely on your seat bones, you are also likely to become sore. Correct your position if you think that could be the cause—ask a friend, or better still, your instructor, to comment on it, and ways in which to improve.

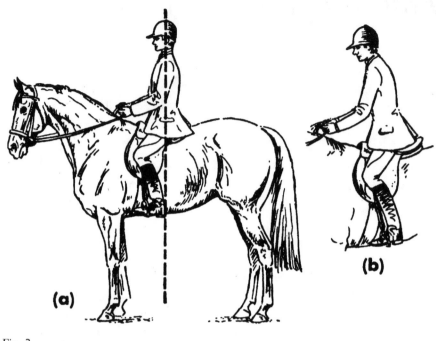

Fig. 3.
(a) Rider in the correct position.
(b) Rider in an incorrect position.

Q. I ride as a hobby, and enjoy looking after my own horse, finding that together with riding him, it is a really enjoyable way of keeping fit. The trouble is, it does seem to be making my muscles rather large and prominent, and I dislike looking unfeminine.

A. Unfortunately, looking after horses is a job which requires physical exertion, and the toning up and development of the muscles from doing so is an occupational hazard. The only solution is to put the horse in a boarding stable so that someone else looks after it and takes on all the heavier jobs—such as mucking out and carrying bales of bedding around—which are building up your muscles.

Q. My pony is stabled all the time, and is very fresh and difficult to handle when I ride him. He fidgets and jogs everywhere even when I only want him to walk, and this is very tiring. Are there some schooling aids which will make him more obedient?

A. This pony is less in need of schooling aids than of a change in stable management. Turn him out for at least a few hours every day so that he has a chance to unwind mentally, and work off any freshness. Make sure that you are not overfeeding him for the amount of exercise you give him, and reduce or cut out altogether any grains that could cause him to get even more excitable. Have an experienced person check the fit of his tack too, so you can be sure that he is not merely reacting to pain.

You might find it beneficial to spend some time quietly schooling at home, teaching him to accept and respond to the contact of your leg, rather than evading it by rushing away. Taking your legs off his sides and pulling at the reins will only make the situation worse, as he will pull back in return and become uptight. When you are riding with a group of other horses, try and keep him at the front, either on his own, or abreast of another person, so that he does not feel that he is in a race and has to chase after a tail in front of him. Keep your legs quietly in contact with his sides, to keep him active and using his hindquarters, so that he takes up a positive contact with the bit.

Q. Whenever my pony is standing still, she paws continually at the ground with a front foot—how do I stop her?

A. This sounds like a bad habit that she has been allowed to get into. It may spring from impatience to be on the move again, but is nevertheless very ill-mannered. It could be potentially dangerous if someone is standing nearby. Each time she does this, scold her, and use your crop on the shoulder of the offending leg. When she does stand quietly, reward her with a pat and a kind word. It may take a little while to correct the habit, but provided you are firm and persevere, she should learn that it is far more pleasant to behave herself.

Q. I've just bought a four-year-old gelding, but he seems to be terribly clumsy and wobbly, although in other respects he is good-natured and well behaved. Is this a physical defect, or will it get better after a while?

A. You should certainly call your vet if you think that there is any physical problem causing lack of balance and coordination, but it sounds more likely that it is simply due to his age. A four-year-old is not the best-balanced animal in the world, and has to learn how to readjust his balance to cope with the unaccustomed weight of a rider. With schooling and time, his coordination and strength should improve, so that you have a more maneuverable and balanced ride. Until this happens, you should use brush boots on him so that he does not injure himself by moving a little awkwardly. Make sure your own position is not throwing him off balance.

Q. My pony won't lead. He hangs back all the time so that I have to drag him along, and if he doesn't feel like going somewhere, he just digs his heels in and stands still.

A. Try carrying a short crop with you, holding it in your left hand with the end of the lead rope or reins. Stand midway between your pony's eye and shoulder, and firmly give the command to "walk on." If he won't oblige, bring the crop around behind your back, and use it in the girth region. This should have the effect of making him go forward; walk on beside him, encouraging him with your voice and stick if necessary. Do not get in front of his eye, or start tugging at him, as it is more likely to create, rather than overcome, resistance.

Fig. 4. How to encourage a reluctant pony to lead.

Q. I have a problem with my boots when riding. I cannot afford custom-made leather boots, but the rubber off-the-shelf variety flap around my calves. When I ride without stirrups, they continually slide down, and I have to keep stopping in order to pull them back up. Is there anything I can do about this?

A. A number of different brands of rubber riding boots are now made in different calf-width fittings, as well as foot sizes, so it is worth trying on several types to find the ones which are the best fit. In the summer, jodhpur boots provide a cooler alternative to long boots, and you will not have the same problem. In the winter, when you will wish to wear your long boots, wear an extra pair of thick socks inside. If the foot of the boot is not large enough to allow room for this, just put on a pair of legwarmers instead. You could also stitch a loop of leather into the top of the back seam of the boots, through which you can thread spur, or boot straps, which are then buckled around your legs.

Q. How can I tell when my horse is on the correct canter lead? I am never really sure—and is it that important anyway?

A. Your horse should appear to be taking longer strides with his inside foreleg, i.e., the one that is to the inside of the bends he is taking, when he is on the correct canter lead. This enables him to stay better balanced on turns. Try running a small circle yourself, on your own two feet, taking first short strides and then long strides with your inside leg, and you will soon appreciate the difference that it makes to him in being able to keep his balance. With practice you will eventually be able to feel which leg he is leading (taking longer strides) with, but it will take a little time and perseverance to acquire the knack. Whenever you ask for canter, first of all try and decide whether it is the correct leg or not, and then check by glancing downward at the shoulders. Do not actually lean over to one side, or you will unbalance your horse, and if you are in a showing or dressage competition, it looks very obvious and unprofessional. Simply glance down—the shoulder will swing further forward on the side to which the foreleg is leading. If on the wrong leg for the direction you are going, trot or walk him, and ask again.

Q. I am rather short, and have a lot of trouble mounting because of this. It is very embarrassing having to struggle on board in front of other people, and I dread having to dismount for any reason when I am out riding.

A. It is possible to buy extending stirrup leathers that will help solve your problems while you're out riding, should you need to dismount. If someone is around, ask for a leg up—this is far better than having to heave yourself on board, which can damage the horse's back or saddle. Failing this, make a mounting block at

Fig. 5. Giving someone a leg up.

home; one can be made quite easily from a few concrete blocks and cement. When away from home, you can always make use of gates and logs from which to mount if you really get stuck. If you are a little overweight, slimming down can help. Unless you have a specific physical problem limiting your suppleness, you can limber up a little by using the following dismounted exercise. Put one foot on the seat of a chair placed in front of you. Then turn the foot which is on the ground so that it is at right angles to the chair, and slowly lean forward so that your weight moves forward over the raised leg. Repeat it with the other leg so that you do not become one-sided when riding.

Q. I seem to have an awful lot of trouble controlling my feet. They seem to keep sliding forward, and my feet slip right through the stirrups, or I lose them altogether, no matter how hard I try to keep the iron on the ball of my foot. How can I keep them in the right place?

Fig. 6. A leg-stretching exercise.

A. Most of this problem stems from stiffness, which prevents you from acquiring a deeper seat. Instead of sitting into the saddle and being able to use your legs independently, you are probably locking your joints, gripping with your knees, and pushing onto your toes.

When you first mount, sit in the center of the saddle, with your feet free of the stirrups. Lift both legs slightly away to each side, holding the front arch of the saddle to help you keep your balance, and then settle them back into the correct position. This should be with your ankle and knee joints flexed so that the knees turn slightly away from the saddle flap, and so that when you look down, you cannot see the toes of each foot past the front of the kneecaps. Place your feet carefully back in the stirrups, and if your legs are in the right place, the leathers should hang down vertically from the stirrup bars.

Try not to ride with your stirrups too long, or you will aggravate, not improve, the situation. It is often better to start off with slightly shorter stirrups and slowly let them down as you become more supple and able to sit deeper into the saddle. Allow your ankle joints to relax, and the heel to sink downward, so that your foot does not slip through the stirrup—but do not force the heel down so hard that the lower leg shoots forward. A pair of rubber treads fitted to the stirrups will also reduce the problem of your feet slipping through them. If possible, you should also try and get a few lessons; it always helps to have constructive criticism from someone on the ground who can see exactly what is going wrong and offer advice on correcting it.

Q. I have just started riding, and am having a lot of trouble with the posting, or rising, trot. I can manage it for a little while, but then I find that I lose my balance. Am I doing something wrong?

A. This is a very common problem among novice riders, but with time and practice it will improve, so that after a while you will wonder what all the fuss was about. It is best if you can practice the rising trot on a horse with a fairly active gait, and which also moves with a reasonably constant tempo. If it is constantly stopping and starting, then you may have trouble picking up the rhythm and falling into the movement. Once you have acquired more coordination, you will find it easier to use your legs to keep this type going, but for the moment, you need something that will keep going at reasonable speed without too much encouragement. Try and allow the bouncy movement of the horse's back to do some of the work for you. Incline your upper body slightly forward, and allow your hips to be pushed in an upward and forward direction as you feel the horse's back begin to throw your seat in the air. Then gently allow your seat to sink down, and start again. A good exercise to practice is to hover with your seat raised slightly out of the saddle. You will probably need to take a handful of mane so that you can keep your balance more easily. Flex your ankles and knees so they work as shock absorbers, and try to find a position where you are sufficiently balanced so you won't need to hang onto the mane too tightly. Maintain this position for a few strides, and then continue in the "up-down" rising movement, and then

Fig. 7. A hovering exercise.

repeat. When you have your lessons with your instructor, discuss your problem, as there are plenty of other things which would also help.

Q. I seem to have trouble finding the right length of stirrup. How long should it be?

A. The length of the stirrup depends on both the activity you are engaged in, and your standard of riding. Generally speaking, when working on the flat, you should ride with as long a stirrup as possible, so that as much of your leg as possible is in contact with the horse's sides. When jumping, your stirrups will need to be shortened, by perhaps as much as three or four holes to allow you to go forward with him over a jump. If you are galloping, a length somewhere between these two is about right to enable you to raise your seat from the saddle in order to stay forward over the center of gravity and free the horse's back. The other factor affecting the length of stirrup you ride with is your standard of riding; the more advanced you are, the longer the stirrup you will be able to cope with. More novice riders need slightly shorter stirrups, particularly when learning to do the rising trot. To gauge your approximate length of stirrup before mounting, place the fingertips of one hand on the stirrup bar, and lift the stirrup up beneath your armpit; the leather should lie along the length of your arm. Once actually mounted, you may need to adjust this slightly, either longer or shorter to suit your needs.

Q. My horse is very stubborn; she does not like to leave other horses, which can create problems when I want to go out on my own. Should I use my

Fig. 8. Checking the length of stirrup leathers.

crop, or try and coax her? I don't want to spoil her by doing the wrong thing.

A. Stubbornness is quite common in young horses, and is a habit that should be nipped in the bud before it becomes more established and difficult to correct. Even a normally well-behaved horse, however, can become particularly attached to another, and can be reluctant to leave it. A weak and ineffective rider can encourage a horse to take advantage of the situation. Whatever you do, though, you should not dismount and lead her, but rather try and ride through the problem instead. Do not tip forward, but sit up straight, or if necessary, with the upper body slightly behind the vertical to give you more push. Use your legs firmly, and keep a proper rein contact; when she begins to dig her heels in, you may need to use your crop or whip to reinforce the request. Use your voice too, and persevere until she obeys you. If you adopt these strong tactics, she will eventually give in.

Some horses try to whip around and turn back, and if you are not quick enough to stop this from happening, you should turn her in a couple of short circles, and then point her back in the direction you wish to go, still urging her strongly onward. When riding in company, instead of always following, ride alongside someone. Gradually push her on until you are taking the lead, and be ready to get after her the instant you feel any reluctance. Hesitation will be interpreted as weakness on your part. Try to avoid doing things that will encourage unresponsiveness—not just following others, but habits such as always cantering toward a gate. When out riding, never turn and retrace your footsteps, but try and find a circular route instead.

Q. I only ride once a week, at a local riding school. Each time I start the lesson, I find I am so stiff that it takes me a long time to loosen up enough to gain any real benefit. Are there any exercises I could do that would help me to stay supple during the rest of the week when I am unable to ride?

A. It can be really helpful for the occasional rider to use some dismounted exercises in between lessons. It will reduce the amount of time taken to loosen up when first getting back in the saddle, and you will be less likely to ache as much the next day. They need not take up a great deal of time; indeed, many can easily be worked in around household chores, while sitting at an office desk, or even while watching television. They could also be used as a means of limbering up just prior to a lesson. Here are a few exercises:

Head rolling: Excellent for relaxing tension in the neck. Allow the head to tilt forward so that the chin rests on the chest, and gently and slowly roll the head from side to side.

Shoulder shrug: Hunch both the shoulders up beneath the ears, breathing in at the same time. Then roll the shoulders back and downward, breathing out again.

Arm circling: Slowly circle each arm in turn through a backward circle, stretching up through the rib cage as the arm moves above the head, and rolling the shoulders back and downward as the arms come to rest by the side of the body.

Elbow push: Hold both arms, elbows bent and fingertips lightly touching, in front of the rib cage at chest height. Push both elbows backward as far as they will go, keeping the arms parallel to the ground.

Wrist suppling: Rotate the wrist joints. Let the hands and fingers relax downward, and gently shake them up and down and also sideways, trying to keep the rest of the forearm fairly steady.

Waist: Hold both arms out to the sides at shoulder height, with the palms uppermost. Swing them around the body, rotating from the waist. Keep the arms in a straight line with each other. Keep the feet spread slightly apart. Then reach down and touch each foot in turn with the fingers of the opposite hand. After that, allow the arms to hang by the sides, and reach down the side of each leg in turn, as far as possible, by inclining the body over in that direction.

Thigh stretch: Set one foot on a chair placed just in front of you. Turn the foot on the ground so that it is at right angles to the chair. Then lean forward so that your weight moves forward over the raised knee.

Ankle circling: While sitting down, rotate the ankle joints in both directions.

Lower legs: Stand at arm's length from a wall, resting the palms of each hand on its surface. Bend the elbows so that the body inclines forward, keeping the heels flat on the floor. Then push the body away again, until upright once more.

These exercises are, on the whole, more beneficial when performed slowly; if there are any physical disabilities, then a doctor should be consulted first before attempting them. Attention should also be paid to normal posture, making an effort not to slouch or round the shoulders. It is also best to avoid crossing the legs, as this can lead to uneven muscular development, and crookedness when riding.

Q. My horse will never canter on the correct leg on the left rein. How can I make him do it properly?

A. There may be a number of reasons why your horse is having problems. If he has been checked over and there are no physical causes, then you will have to put in some extra work on his school-

Fig. 9. The canter sequence, with the right "off" fore leading.

ing to try and correct it. Always ask for the canter in a place where his balance is such as to predispose him to striking off correctly—either on a circle or in a corner—when you have established a correct bend to the inside. Throughout the entire transition, you will have to maintain this bend. Stiff horses will frequently try and evade it if they are allowed, so you may need to be very firm and positive. Most will try to avoid cantering on the difficult lead by bending to the outside, propping weight onto the inside shoulder, and swinging the quarters outward. All your aids need to be directed at preventing this. Keep the outside leg drawn firmly backwards to control the quarters, and raise the inside hand a little to help maintain bend and prevent the weight from being dropped onto the inside shoulder. If you are able to, push the quarters inward a little bit, so that the outside hind leg (the first one to push off into canter) is really engaged strongly. Each time you get a wrong transition, stop and try again. It may take time, but persevere, rewarding your horse with a pat and plenty of praise when he gets it right, and you will soon find he becomes more consistent.

Q. My pony is rather lazy, and never goes forward into another pace when I want him to. He shuffles along a bit faster, and eventually breaks into the pace—but it isn't really the instant response to my leg signals that I would like!

A. Buy a dressage whip to reinforce your leg signals. Get him as active as possible in each gait; if his quarters are engaged well underneath him, he will be better prepared to spring forward into the next one. Although this means that you will need to use plenty of leg, try to avoid being punishing with them, or else his sides will grow numb after a while, and he will stop taking any notice of you at all. If you find that you do not get enough response when you apply your legs, rather than kicking, use them again and at the same time give him a little flick with the whip just behind your calf. Practice riding lots of transitions one after the other to keep him alert and on his toes. Use small circles (between 10 and 15 yards in diameter) to get him using his back end more.

Q. Each time I ask for canter, my horse just rushes off, and can often be quite difficult to stop again. Should I persevere, or keep canter work to a minimum so that he doesn't get worked up?

A. It is best to spend more time working on the canter, so that it becomes accepted as work, rather than as a good excuse for mis-behaving or a show of temperament. Be careful not to be overly severe with the leg aids, and think of the best ways in which to approach the problem. Cantering for long periods of time, for example, will give him the chance to take charge, so canter work is best divided into relatively short periods, doing other work in between. A good exercise would be to set yourself a certain number of strides in each gait, e.g., ten strides trot, ten strides canter, ten strides trot, and so on. Increasing or decreasing the number of strides will vary the degree of difficulty, and prevent him from anticipating. It will, however, deny him the chance for just taking off, and will get him in the frame of mind where he is waiting for a command to slow down. Riding this exercise on a circle will add to the steadying effect.

Q. My horse leans on my hands so much that my arms really ache. He carries his head very low too; is there some way of improving his head carriage so that he is less tiring to ride?

A. Leaning on the hands can be due to bad conformation, teeth trouble, being on the forehand (most of the weight supported over the front legs), or it could be a resistance to the bit and/or the rider's hands. Conformation cannot be changed. The mouth should be checked by a vet. Schooling can be worked on, though, to improve the head carriage. A horse that is on its forehand often tends to carry its head rather low, and then leans on the rider's hands as a means of helping to balance itself. Use plenty of transitions and some occasional work over poles on the ground to get him engaging his quarters as much as possible. As he begins to move his back legs beneath his body weight more, he'll then support himself on his shoulders and front legs less, and the head carriage will become slightly higher. Be careful not to rush him too fast, as this will only undo your schooling work. If he is leaning on your hands out of resistance, you should try to make your arms as flexible as possible. If they are stiff and unyielding, he will only lean against you more. Keep the elbows bent and the wrists slightly rounded so that you are able to follow the movements of his head and neck better.

By moving the third fingers slightly on the reins, you can create a little movement in the bit which will also discourage him from leaning—although this should never become a sawing motion, just a barely perceptible movement. A change of bit might also help. A wire- or ring-snaffle bit, or one with rollers, will be less fixed in his mouth and more difficult to evade in this manner. Check that he is not opening his mouth or crossing his jaws at the same time; a change of nose band or an adjustment to the existing one may be needed if he is.

Q. My pony will not stand still while I am trying to mount him. How can I make him behave—he just walks off without me!

A. No horse or pony will stand quietly if it is in any pain or discomfort, so be sure that his tack fits properly, and he is quite sound. Consider the way in which you are mounting, which could be promoting his behavior. Have both of the reins gathered up in your left hand to give you a firm enough contact to stop him walking forward, but not so tight that you pull him backwards. Both reins should be the same length; if one is shorter than the other he will be pulled off balance and have to move around to regain it. He should also be standing squarely, so that he is able to balance himself against the weight of a rider mounting from one side. Take a good handful of mane in the left hand together with the reins. This will help stop you from accidentally pulling on one or both of them, and will give you something firm to pull on should you need it—not something which is likely to move, as the saddle could. When putting your foot in the stirrup, do not dig a toe in his side, but put the foot in the stirrup right up to the instep, so that you can point the toe downward.

When actually mounting, take hold of the pommel, or the flap of the saddle, rather than the cantle. If you take the back of the saddle, you are likely to pull it over toward yourself, make the horse's back sore, and twist the wooden framework inside the saddle. Spring up with plenty of agility; the more slowly you go about it, the more difficult your horse will find it to balance himself. When you land in the saddle, try to land gently, rather than like a ton of lead, and do not suddenly clamp your legs onto his sides. Whenever he moves, scold him, dismount and start again. When he is good, praise him generously. You might find that it will help at first if you can persuade someone to hold him for you. With time, and by sharpening up your mounting technique, he should learn to behave himself.

3

Equitation—Jumping

Q. I am entering my horse for some cross-country competitions this year, and am working at getting him fit. I am finding, though, that even looking after and riding him myself, I am not very fit, getting out of breath very quickly when we are jumping. I don't want to let him down—are there any other things I can do to improve my fitness?

A. First, part of the problem may be due to your holding your breath while jumping—it is a common problem for many people, and will invariably leave you short of breath. Talking, singing, or counting to yourself quietly will help to get you breathing more normally. To improve your general level of fitness, you could try jogging, although if you do not find this very enjoyable, there are plenty of other ways; skipping or playing tennis are both very good, and also help to develop concentration, coordination, and the speed of the reflexes, all of which are important when riding cross-country. Bicycling will also help to get you more fit, and you could try swimming as a way to increase lung capacity.

Q. My pony is really bad about having his bridle put on, so I have been riding him in his halter instead. Would it be safe to jump him in a halter?

A. It is not safe to ride in a halter by itself at any time, let alone to try jumping in one. It is more important to look into the cause of his being difficult to bridle up, and deal with that instead. If it is a physical problem, but one which should not stop you from riding, you could use a hackamore temporarily until the problem is cleared up.

Q. My pony won't jump anything over 2 feet, and is also lazy and clumsy when jumping, often knocking fences down. Would athletic jumping help him?

A. Some horses and ponies just are not natural athletes, and a few even seem to have a built-in tape measure, so that it is impossible to persuade them to jump higher than the limit they have set for themselves. Age is also another factor to take into consideration; a youngster may be green and uncoordinated, while an old horse may be stiff and unable to perform very athletically anymore. Gymnastic exercises are only really beneficial in helping to improve the technique of the animal; it will not enable him to jump any higher, and unless approached with care, would be physically unfair on an older horse, and may upset a younger one not yet ready. For this reason, and also because it means you do not have to keep getting on and off to adjust fences, it is best if such training is done under the supervision of someone experienced in such matters.

If your pony is normally lazy, and not just when jumping, you might reexamine your feeding program. If he is provided with a little more energy, he may well begin to approach all his work with a little more zest and enthusiasm. If he really does lack ability, and does not enjoy jumping as much as you do, you may be better off in the long run to try something else instead, such as dressage or long-distance riding.

Q. I would really love to do more jumping, but it absolutely terrifies me. I start to lose my balance, and then I tend to panic!

A. The answer to this is to not attempt to do too much before you are really ready. You need to build your confidence up slowly, taking things in easy stages. Start off with just a single pole on the ground, and walk, trot, and canter over this with your stirrups at jumping length. You will soon get used to gauging your distance from it as you approach, and your horse is unlikely to put in a huge and unseating leap over it—just a gentle hop at the most. Lean forward slightly as you pass over the pole, so that you begin to condition yourself to going forward with the horse rather than fighting against it and instinctively leaning backwards. Keep your heels deep, move your seat slightly back in the saddle, and push your hands forward slightly, allowing your horse to stretch his neck out, but without losing the rein contact, so that your upper body folds forward over the horse's neck from the hips. This makes for a very secure position, and you will get used to slipping into it at the right moment with practice.

Once you are happy with your progress over one pole on the ground, raise it to a height of about a foot, and once more trot and canter over it. Hold a handful of mane on the approach if you like, so that you have something to help keep you forward, and to hang onto if you feel you really need it. Do remember to keep looking ahead, and not down at the ground, otherwise you will lose your balance and get left behind. Keep using plenty of leg to maintain the pace—the better your horse is going forward to meet the jump, the more comfortable it will all feel to you. He will probably only hop over this jump, just giving you enough of a feeling that he has left the ground. Only when you feel quite happy about going over it should you make it any larger—do not feel that you have to keep up with your friends. Jumping should be fun for both horse and rider, and you are the best judge as to what height you feel happiest about jumping.

Q. Every time I get to a jump, my pony seems to hesitate, and then jumps it at the last minute, just when I least expect it, which is very unsettling. Is there any way of improving her style, so that it is more comfortable?

A. There are several points to consider here; she may be frightened of receiving a jab in the mouth, especially if she is wearing a strong bit such as a pelham or a Kimberwicke. Change to a less damaging, milder bit if required, and try to adopt a better position where you are not hanging onto the reins. If you need to, take hold of a handful of mane or the pommel, so that you do not get left behind and inadvertently take a tug on the reins. If you land heavily on her back, then it will also make her uncomfortable and unwilling to jump freely, in case you land even more heavily. If your pony has an excitable nature, there is also a possibility that you are holding her back so strongly that she is unable to jump fluently. If she is very stiff, she may need to be allowed to move on a bit faster than others in order to clear the jump. If she is a little lazy, she will need to be pushed on more strongly toward her fences so that she tackles them more positively. You could be partly to blame for this; do not freeze at the last minute, but try and ride on, both before, over, and after, the fence. She will need this help particularly if she is a short-striding pony, as this type tends to take off and land very close to their fences unless ridden on very vigorously. Do be careful not to overface her either. If you are jumping fences that are too much on the high side for her ability, then an awkward jump is only to be expected, and if you persist she may start refusing.

Q. My horse has started to refuse at jumps; I have owned him for a year and competed very successfully at shows with him all this summer with no problems whatsoever. Now, all of a sudden, it is a real struggle to get him over even the smallest jump.

A. This sounds as though your horse has been overjumped. He has evidently done quite a bit of competition work recently, and doubtless has practiced at home too. Forget about jumping for the moment, and place the emphasis on letting him enjoy himself; go out for some rides, and just do a little flatwork to keep him supple and his mind active. The ground can be pretty hard in the summer, and if it has been jarring his legs, then this will also make him understandably reluctant to jump. Once he has had a complete break from jumping, you might find that taking him hunting during the winter will help to restore his enthusiasm for jumping again. When returning to competition work, be selective, rather than overjumping him—and try not to practice too much at home.

Q. My horse has got quite a jump—the trouble being that he doesn't always jump clear. Although he is quite capable, he seems to get a bit lazy and will keep brushing against a fence every now and then, even though he could clear it easily if he tried. How can I make him tuck his feet up more?

A. Athletic jumping often helps to improve jumping technique; teaching your horse to tuck his feet up out of the way, and to position himself correctly over the fence. Unless you are very experienced, though, it is best to go to a good instructor for such instruction, as it is easy to do a great deal of damage, and shake the confidence if distances have been wrongly set up. Distances over fences and poles need to be varied slightly according to each animal's length of stride and what you are trying to achieve, and it does take a good eye and a certain amount of experience to judge what is right. It does sound quite likely in your horse's case, though, that his jumping abilities are not so much at fault as his attitude. Don't practice at home, but keep him fresh for shows instead, just popping over the practice fence a couple of times to warm up before the class. That way he will go into the ring taking a good look at everything, and making more of an effort. Too much work over jumps at home will only make him switch off and become rather bored with it all—but you can keep working on his flatwork so that he remains supple and obedient.

Q. Every time my horse lands after a jump he puts his head right down, shaking it from side to side and putting in little bucks. I have fallen off several times because of this—is there any way of stopping him?

A. This may be due to either an over-strong or insufficient contact. If it is too strong, then he may well be trying to find some freedom from it on landing, when you are in a less secure position. If it is insufficient, then he may just be taking advantage of the moment to indulge in a little high spirits. Try and develop a more secure position so that you are able to adjust your rein contact to suit you both better. The best way of doing this is to have some lessons at a riding school on a steady horse, and in an enclosed area, so that you can work without your stirrups, and perhaps without your reins too. When jumping your own horse, make sure that you do not give him a chance to idle after jumping a fence. Keep a firm but steady contact on landing, sit up and ride positively away, rather than waiting for the worst. You might even find that placing a second fence after the first, or having to negotiate a turn will get him concentrating more on the work at hand, and less on playing about. Do not rule out the possibility that his saddle may be causing him discomfort, or that his back may be twingeing as he uses it over a jump; ask your an expert or your vet to check out these possibilities.

Q. My three-year-old is coming along nicely on the flat, and I would now like to teach her to jump. How do I go about this, or should I wait until she is a bit older?

A. At three years old, the bones are still very immature, and if overstressed could be permanently damaged. Leave jumping until she is four, when you can begin to introduce her first to a single pole on the ground, and then to lines of three poles at equal distances from each other. The distance apart may vary from about 4 feet, 3 inches to 5 feet, according to her natural length of stride and height. If she has to fit in the occasional hop or half stride, they are too far apart, while if the stride becomes stilted, they are too close together. When the distance is correct, there should be no difference in the stride, other than an increased degree of elevation and activity, and a lowering of the head and neck. When she is working calmly over these in a trot, introduce a small crossrail fence with a single pole just in front of it. This will need to be positioned approximately 9 feet away from the fence. Using a crossrail as the obstacle will help to get her into the habit of jumping straight, and at the center of the fence. It should be kept fairly low to start with—about 12 to 18 inches at the center will be sufficient. Once quite confident and quietly trotting over this sort of jump, you can progress to small verticals of about 2 feet to 2 feet, 6 inches. Rather than increase the height, try to change the type of jump, so that she becomes used to variety, and learns to take it all in her stride. You could begin to do some jumping from a canter too, (remove the pole on the approach), and when you feel she is ready, introduce some small spreads. Even at this age, she will be more susceptible to injury than a more mature horse, and you should try and avoid doing too much, especially when the ground is hard. Jumping practice can be restricted to perhaps twice a week—you do not want her to become bored by it either. Once she is five, you can begin to concentrate more seriously on her jumping if she shows talent in that direction, and give her some experience in small jumping classes. But it is worth taking it slowly and steadily while she is still young.

Q. I keep falling off when I am jumping, usually just as my horse is landing. He seems almost to slow down, and his head seems very low, so that I lose my balance. I am covered in bruises, and getting very discouraged. How can I stay on top?

A. Two things need to be done; your position must be improved, and you must ride on more energetically as you are landing. Keep your heels deep, and watch that your lower leg does not slip backwards, which will otherwise make your position weak and unbalanced. Sit up more quickly as you land, and you should then find it easier to both stay on board and rebalance him so that his head does not seem so low. You will also find it easier to use your legs, which will correct his head carriage a little; it will also make him move away from the fence more quickly on landing, so that you do not end up with him stopping, and you continuing on your own.

Q. My horse tries to rush off each time we land after a fence, so that it is really difficult to turn in time for the next jump when I am in a competition. How can I slow him down a bit?

A. Be careful that you are not landing in the saddle with a crash each time you land, otherwise your horse may try to run away from the anticipated pain. He sounds like the enthusiastic type who is eager to get on with the job at hand. This means that you will need to speed up your own reactions if you are to remain in control. If your reins are in loops as he lands, he is bound to get away from you, so keep a firm contact throughout all phases of the jump. You must know the course thoroughly, and be ready to give him instructions about where he is going next, otherwise he will take things into his own hands. When schooling at home, you could try jumping him through doubles, or placing a pole between 21 to 24 feet away on the landing side, to encourage him to steady a little and think about where he is going.

Q. My horse often takes off too far away from the jump, which takes me by surprise. When jumping spreads, it also means that he often knocks the back pole down; is there any method of getting him to take off closer?

A. When schooling, avoid ramp oxers. Use either vertical fences, or true spreads, with the front and back poles at the same height. Make sure that there is some kind of groundline, and that it is not pulled forward (toward the horse) in front of the jump. Do not approach too fast, but keep a steady pace, and look toward either the center or bottom of the fence, not out over the top of it. If you have the occasional jumping lesson, ask your instructor to show you the right distance at which to place a pole on the ground in front of the jump to encourage him to take off closer to it. Working over jumps in a trot will also encourage him to get closer before taking off.

Q. My pony jumps very crookedly, so that when we are jumping in-and-outs or double or triple combinations, he goes so far across to the left that he either runs out, or bumps my foot on the wings. How can I straighten this out?

A. School at home over some crossrails—this will keep him more centered, and make him tuck his feet up beneath himself rather than twisting them to one side. You could also put up a diagonal pole from the left side of the fence to try and keep him approaching the middle. Carry your crop or whip in your left hand, and when you feel him beginning to swing across in that direction, use it on that shoulder. Be ready to use your seat and legs more on

Fig. 10. A suitable fence to help correct a horse which jumps crookedly across to the left.

each approach to keep him straight. If he jumps crookedly, it will not only prove injurious to one or the other of you, but it means that he is less likely to be able to clear a wide spread, and will make the distance between combinations longer than it should be.

4

Saddlery and Horse Clothing

Q. When I am riding, I can hear a strange, creaking noise. I can't hear it at any other time—is this a problem with my horse or my saddlery?

A. It sounds as though you should check the saddle over. New saddles do sometimes squeak a lot, so give it a good application of neat's-foot, or some proprietary brand of saddle oil. If, however, this saddle is not new, then the noise could be due to a broken tree inside it; this is constructed of beechwood reinforced at points with steel, and is very prone to damage if the saddle is dropped or otherwise mishandled. A broken tree is eventually going to damage your horse's back, so take it to a tack shop to be checked over.

Q. My saddle recently got soaked in a rainstorm. I oiled and then soaped it, but the surface seems to have become furry and spongy on the seat. As it is an expensive saddle and I have tried to look after it, I'd like to try to restore it. Is there a special preparation I can use?

A. The condition described usually only occurs if the leather has become oversaturated with water, and the fibers begin to separate.

Whenever leather gets soaked it should be washed to remove any dirt and then allowed to dry naturally in a cool, rather than warm, place. Once it is completely dry, it can then be oiled thoroughly to restore any grease it has lost. This should not be done while it is still damp, otherwise the oil will not penetrate (oil and water do not mix, and the oil would just sit in a film on the surface and do no good at all). The best thing that you can do with your saddle is to ignore it for a while. Rather than using further preparations, just give it a wipe over with a damp cloth after use, but stop oiling it at all, and let it dry out until the seat is hard and shiny, when you can treat it as normal again.

Q. I recently purchased a new black saddle, and soon discovered that the dye keeps coming out of it—the seat of my jodhpurs become black every time I ride. I've tried washing the leather thoroughly, but it doesn't seem to make any difference. The tack shop I bought it from won't change it, and said to keep washing it. What should I do? I can't afford to buy another saddle, and I am quite happy with this one in other respects.

A. Follow the advice you have already been given. It is not the fault of the tack shop, but rather of whoever processed the leather initially. The dye will normally tend to come out of any leather that has been colored, unless it has been given a plasticized surface, and black dye is particularly unstable. Even when buying new saddlery that has not been dyed, you should still give it a thorough wash before use, as water-based dyes are also used along raw edges where the leather has been cut. Otherwise the dye will be washed out upon the hair if the horse becomes sweaty or the leather wet, which could be disastrous in a showing class. Continue to wash the saddle after each use, using fairly hot water with a little dishwashing liquid added to it, so that you remove as much of the dye as possible; oil and soap it afterwards each time so that the leather does not dry out, but begins to take on its own natural color.

Q. My four-year-old mare is difficult to get a bridle on; she just won't open her mouth to take the bit. When she does, she then puts her head right up in the air so that I can't reach to put the headpiece over her ears. Is there any way of making her more cooperative?

A. Ask your vet to rule out any possibility of physical problems, which might include sharp teeth, ulcers, lampas, or an ear infection; or at her age she may well be teething and feeling some discomfort because of it. Make sure that the bridle and bit are also comfortable, since all these factors will contribute to awkwardness. If there are no physical problems, ensure that you are completely blameless for her behavior—avoid banging her teeth with the bit when putting the bridle on or taking it off, as this will make her less than cooperative. You might also try holding a few pieces of carrot, or horse and pony cubes, together with the bit on the palm of your hand to encourage her to open her mouth and consider it all as being a pleasant experience.

If she does not improve after making these allowances, she is simply being a little naughty, and you should try to place yourself in a position which gives you greater control while putting the bridle on. Stand beside your mare, holding the bit on the palm of your left hand. Encircle her nose with your right arm, holding the cheekpieces of the bridle in your right hand. If she tries to raise her head you will then be able to prevent her by pressing down on her nose with your right hand. Offer the bit on the palm of your left hand; if she won't open her mouth, slide your thumb in at the corner where there are no teeth, and press it down on her tongue. As she opens her mouth, quickly slip the bit in and raise the cheekpieces upward with your right hand so that it does not slip out again. Then use your left hand to push her ears through the headpiece. If you are fairly short, try standing on an overturned bucket or box (something fairly stable) so that you have the advantage of height as well.

Fig. 11. Putting on a bridle.

Q. *The leg straps on my horse's turnout blanket seem to rub him a lot—he gets very sore around his back legs and a lot of the hair has been rubbed away. Would it be better to cut the straps off completely?*

A. If you do this, the blanket is very likely to slip if he rolls, which could be more dangerous than leaving the straps on; the back may also flap forward if it is windy, leaving him with little protection from the cold and wet, and possibly frightening him into the bargain. Make sure that you are not fastening them too tightly, and if they are made of leather, keep them clean and well oiled so that they are soft, supple, and less likely to chafe. Nylon straps should also be kept as clean as possible. Check the blanket at least twice each day—if it has slipped, straighten it; otherwise, this will eventually cause soreness around the shoulders as well as around the legs. The leg straps can be lined by slipping a length of bicycle tire inner tubing or washable synthetic fleece over them. Ideally, you could attach a wide belly band of material similar to your blanket, as is often seen on quilted turnout blankets, and add darts to the back for a better fit, less likely to slip; alternatively, use crossing belly straps and a fillet string or tail cord to replace the leg straps altogether.

Q. My gelding's blankets slip a lot in the stable, and I often find him shivering with cold the next morning. He is clipped and I worry that he will get chilled, but am at a loss as to how to keep everything in place.

A. There are several things which can be done. You may not be tightening the straps sufficiently to hold it firmly in place. Be careful, likewise, not to tighten them so that the horse becomes uncomfortable. If the blanket continues to slide, you could line it with a less slippery material, like flannel or cotton. If this does not work, it may be helpful to attach some leg straps, like those found on a turnout blanket. This may solve the problem, especially if the leg strap on the opposite side to which the rug tends to slip is fastened a little shorter. Another alternative is to attach crossing belly straps on the blanket, which you can use instead of the typical straight surcingles. These do seem to be very successful in keeping blankets in place.

You should also ensure, of course, that the blankets you are using are not causing discomfort because they do not fit properly. Some horses are allergic to certain fibers, which makes them more inclined to try and dislodge them. If the blanket is tailored as much as possible to the shape of the animal, so much the better, you can also ask your tack shop personnel to put darts, a tail guard,

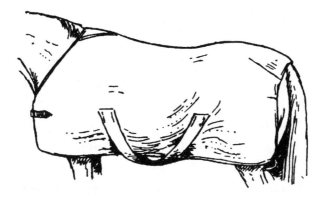

Fig. 12. Crossing belly straps and darts.

or a drawstring over the quarters of it to snug it down. Two breast straps, rather than a single one, also seem to help.

Q. I've got a saddle pad made out of real sheepskin, but it is getting rather dirty. How should I go about cleaning it?

A. If it isn't too grubby, you could sprinkle a little talcum powder on it and then brush it out, as this will absorb some of the sweat and dirt. Look at the label on it too, as some of these saddle pads are washable. If so, use soft soap and warm water, rinsing thoroughly. Allow it to dry naturally, kneading it occasionally to prevent it from becoming stiff. If it is not washable, then you will have to get it dry-cleaned.

Q. My horse lives out all year-round and so has developed a very oily coat to protect himself from the weather. My tack gets very greasy because of this, and it is terrible trying to keep everything clean. Are there any quick ways of getting the grease off? Also, when I have soaped it, the leather always seems to look dull, and never has a nice sheen on it—could I be doing something wrong?

A. Use a thin quilted cotton saddle pad, which will help to protect the saddle lining without actually altering the fit of the saddle. This will be easy to keep clean, as all you need to do is pop it in the washing machine when it gets dirty. When you wash your tack, use a few drops of dishwashing liquid in the water, which also needs to be fairly hot if you are to get rid of all the grease. This will make your job a lot easier; any really stubborn spots of grease can be removed by gently nudging them off with a fingernail. Try and clean your tack fairly frequently; even if you only have time to give it a quick wipe each time it is used, it will still save you from having a mammoth task on your hands at the end of each week. It is important to keep your tack as clean as possible, not just from the point of view of safety and prolonging its life, but also to keep your horse free from sores and galls.

Q. I have always tried to take good care of my saddle, cleaning it every time it is used. I now find, however, that it feels very greasy and unpleasant. How can I correct this?

A. It sounds as though the leather has been overnourished. Wash it thoroughly with very hot, regularly changed, water that has had a few drops of dishwashing liquid added to it. Wash it less often, and use less soap, instead of overdoing it. After riding, wiping it with a damp cloth will be sufficient on most occasions, with more thorough attention once a week.

Q. We have had a lot of saddlery thefts in our area, some from even well-locked tackrooms. Are there any ways in which I can protect my saddlery since, although it is insured, it would still be very inconvenient if it was stolen?

A. You should of course make sure that any rooms used for storage of saddlery are locked and padlocked, and windows are barred or bolted in some manner to make access more difficult. A burglar alarm should also be installed, and you could also security mark your tack. You can mark your tack with your social security, driver's license, or telephone number, using a metal stamp to indent the leather. These should be redone occasionally as they do tend to grow fainter, but can prove to be a means of tracing, and recovering, stolen items. It is effective as a deterrent too, since a label can be stuck up on the wall inside the room, in a prominent position, stating that everything is security marked. Notices to this effect should not, however, be posted outside, nor any other signs which advertise the fact that saddlery is stored there.

Q. I'd like to clip my horse, but have a problem in that he tears his blankets. I can't clip him without blanketing him, as he does feel the cold, but the blankets I put on him are in tatters within minutes. He is desperately in need of clipping as he is getting so hot when I ride, but I can hardly go ahead if I can't keep him warm.

A. There is really only one solution for a horse that tears its blankets, and that is to put a muzzle on him. This can be bought from your tack shop, but you should make sure that the halter you use fits well and won't rub. Although it is possible to use a bucket-type muzzle without a halter, it does make sense to attach it to one, or else it can be easily dislodged over one ear. Look for any obvious reasons for this habit too—ensure that his blankets are not irritating him in any way. If you are over-blanketing him in your anxiety to keep him warm, for example, he may be getting too hot, and will look for ways of removing his clothing. Similarly, if he is uncomfortable because the blankets are a bad fit, or the surcingle or leg straps are too tight, or pinching, he will also look for ways to escape the discomfort.

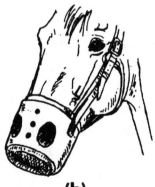

(a)   **(b)**

Fig. 13.
(a) Bib muzzle.
(b) Bucket muzzle.

Q. How should I go about washing my blankets that are ready to put away for next year? And how should they be stored?

A. Brush all the linings first, to remove the worst of the stable stains and any loose hairs. Alternatively, you may prefer to do them in the bathtub, or even in the washing machine, if it is large and sturdy enough. Most synthetic blankets are washable, many by machine, and are less bulky on the whole, but the individual manufacturers' instructions should be followed in such cases.

Turnout blankets can be scrubbed, but detergents should not be used as they are rather harsh, and will remove the waterproofing. Any necessary repairs should be made before storing, which can be done by placing them in large plastic bags with a few mothballs. These can then be labeled so that the contents are identifiable, and they can be placed somewhere dry, such as a loft.

Q. I have just sold my pony, but probably won't get another one for at least a year. I would like to hang onto the saddle and bridle, but am not sure how to go about storing them.

A. Wash the leather first of all, taking everything apart; then condition it with a leather dressing, which will help to prevent it from drying out or becoming moldy. Wrap a sheet around everything to keep the dust out and store somewhere dry, preferably away from direct heat or sunlight. If possible, store the saddle on a wall rack or stand to avoid damage; or else upright, on the pommel.

Q. How often should I get my saddle reflocked?

A. The flocking, or stuffing, inside the panels of the saddle, is usually fairly soft in new saddles. It packs down quite quickly and will need further attention sometime during the first year. After that, it should be checked thoroughly every six months, or at any time when the saddle does not fit the horse, or tips the rider forward or backward. Remember that horses and ponies can change shape quite dramatically according to the amount and type of exercise (or lack of it) they receive, and so this must be taken into account. Sometimes it may be necessary to remove flock, rather than increase it—if the animal has suddenly put on a lot of weight, for example. Occasionally it may be found that the flock has become lumpy, which can cause pressure points on the horse's back, and tender areas as a result; in such cases, all the flocking is removed and replaced.

Q. I am going to buy a horse shortly—what are the basics that I can expect to buy for it?

A. Your requirements will vary according to whether you intend to keep your horse stabled, or living outdoors. You should be able to manage with far less if he lives out, for example. Start off with the essentials, so that you will at least have everything necessary to hand initially, and then later on you can add to them as you wish. If he is to be living out he will need:

- Bridle plus bit (and martingale if required)
- All-Purpose saddle, buckle guards, stirrups
- Girth
- Halter and lead rope
- Turnout blanket
- Grooming tools
- Tack-cleaning equipment
- First Aid kit
- Fly scrim and/or repellent
- Saddle pad

If he is to be stabled, either all or part of the time, he will need in addition:

- Stable blanket
- Cooler
- Anti-sweat sheet
- Mucking-out tools (wheelbarrow, pitchfork, shovel, broom)

Q. I cannot afford to buy a new saddle, and wonder what problems, if any, are attached to buying secondhand tack?

A. This is a difficulty which many people have to face, but often it can be better in the long run to save up the extra money and buy new saddlery if at all possible. Ask a knowledgeable person to come and fit the tack to your horse, which saves a lot of running back and forth, and allows you to try a range of different saddles or blankets in order to find the best fit. It gives you the benefit of an informed and experienced opinion.

It can often be difficult for the inexperienced person to pick out a genuine bargain from the rubbish when buying second-hand. So, if this is the only recourse open to you, you should certainly avoid auctions, and ask an informed person to come along and help advise you. Apart from the obvious problems, such as that the equipment must suit both horse and rider, there can be many other hidden pitfalls. Don't rush into anything if you are not entirely satisfied with it. If major repair work looks to be necessary, buying secondhand can prove to be anything but economical.

Check the state of the leather—it should be firm and greasy, with no signs of wrinkling or blistering. Look carefully at points where the leather has been in contact with metal, such as the bit, stirrups, and buckles, as these may prove to be worn and weakened. If the flaps, seat, or panels of a saddle are very worn, you should take this into account when negotiating a price, as repairing these areas will be costly, and may even look unsightly. Tug gently at any stitching to see if it is safe; re-stitching in most areas does not cost much, but in certain areas such as around the saddle flaps, it is likely to require frequent maintenance. Bridlework which has been backstitched (this looks like one continuous stitch on the reverse side) is usually indicative of poor quality workmanship and cheap materials, and is also very likely to rub. Metal fittings, including buckles and hook studs, should be of good quality, in good condition, and not worn with age.

Indian saddlery should be avoided; the workmanship and design are far better than they were a few years ago, but the materials used still tend to be of inferior quality, and often unsafe. Indian leather can be identified by an unpleasant pungent smell if it is still reasonably new, combined with a distinctive yellowish coloring. It is less pleasant to the touch, may sometimes be heavily grained, and the saddles are often flocked with something resembling multicolored carpet scraps.

Check the girth straps, and the webs that they are attached to; there should be three on each side of the saddle, and they should be in good condition. Replacement is fairly easy if necessary, and may be worthwhile if the saddle is otherwise in good condition, but a reduction in price could be sought on account of the expense. A broken tree (the beechwood framework inside the saddle) is probably one of the more serious hazards to avoid, and can be detected by an excessive amount of movement, and possibly squeaking too, when it is tested by pressing the "points"—or the cantle and pommel—toward each other. This is a test that really needs to be performed by somebody who knows what to look for, as "spring" trees are more flexible than "rigid" ones, and can often be deceptive.

Q. I have just bought a few secondhand blankets—are there any precautions I should take before using them?

A. Before using any secondhand saddlery or horse clothing, you should disinfect it thoroughly first to try and ensure that any skin

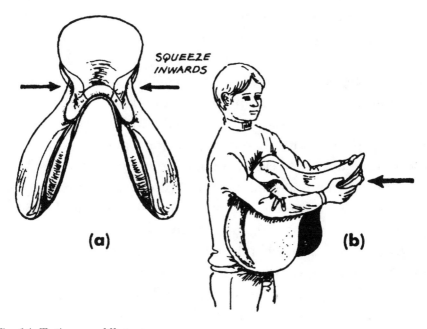

SQUEEZE INWARDS

(a)

(b)

Fig. 14. Testing a saddle tree across:
(a) the front arch, and
(b) the waist.

diseases the last horse or pony may have had are not passed on. You can do this by using a fairly strong sterilizing solution. You should also do the same if your tack has ever gone moldy, as ordinary washing will not kill the spores, which can result in a nasty irritation.

Q. My mare is very bad about having her saddle put on—she hunches her back up and snaps at me while I am trying to tighten up the girth—how can I stop her from doing this?

A. It would be wise to rule out the possibility of any physical discomfort first, by getting the vet or another experienced person to check her back and inspect the fit of the saddle. When putting the saddle on, be careful to place it gently on her back, slightly further forward than necessary, and then to slide it back into position so that all the hairs lie flat and in the right direction beneath. She may be rather sensitive to the initial contact of the saddle, and you may find it helps to use a thicker pad between the saddle and her back. You should pull the front of it well up into the front arch of the saddle so that it doesn't press onto the withers. When tightening the girth, do it firmly but not abruptly, and not excessively. Both of the buckles on each side of the girth should lie level with each other to eliminate the danger of pinching as much as possible. To increase comfort, each of the front legs should be picked up and stretched forward, so that any loose skin or hair is not caught up beneath. After this, walk her around in hand for five minutes or so, to give the saddle time to settle down on her back before tightening the girth completely and mounting. With a more tactful approach, you should find that she will gradually become more amenable.

Q. Every winter, my pony gets rub marks around his withers, on his back where the surcingle goes over his spine, and down the sides of his shoulders. Apart from the fact that this must be rather uncomfortable for him, it takes a long time for the hair to grow out again; in the meantime, the bald patches look awful. Is there any way of preventing this from happening?

A. Make sure that your blankets fit properly; if they are tight around the shoulders they will rub him as he moves around, while if they are prone to slipping, they will rub as they slide round. You could also pad the shoulders with pieces of real or synthetic sheepskin, and stitch two pieces of foam on either side of the withers. This will not only help to keep the blankets from slipping, but will also lift the blanket off the withers, thus preventing rubbing in this area. When stabled, use a thick piece of foam rubber or felt beneath the surcingle to prevent any excessive pressure on the spine, which will make him sore. When he is out in the field in his turnout blanket, stitch a piece of foam into the lining on either side of his spine; this will do the same job, but without the padding becoming lost or muddy. Alternatively, substitute crossing belly straps and a fillet string.

Q. There is a movable catch on the end of the stirrup bar on my saddle; should this be left up or down?

A. There is a difference of opinion over whether this hinge on the stirrup bar should be left up or down. If down, it may allow the stirrup leather to slip off the bar; but some people say that leaving it down permits the stirrup to slip off when the rider falls, thereby saving the rider from being dragged. When the hinge is left up, the stirrup leather is kept in place; if the rider falls, his weight exerts more than enough pressure to cause a well-adjusted hinge to open.

5

Grazing and Fencing

Q. I will be buying a pony soon, and I'm not sure if my field is adequate. How big should it be, and what sort of qualities should it have?

A. It is not always possible to pick and choose your grazing land as much as you would like. Even when you can, it is still far from easy to find a location that could be classed as "perfect." It should, however, be large enough to support the number of animals expected to graze it, otherwise the land will quickly become sour and worm-infested so that it is left not only useless but harmful. You should be able to keep one pony on one acre of land (provided it is regularly rested and properly maintained). Larger areas tend to suffer less from selective grazing and physical damage to the ground, and can normally support about 1,000–1,400 pounds of animal weight per acre if it is in good condition. Make sure that the fencing is in good repair to prevent accidents. Check that there is an adequate, dependable supply of fresh water. You need to refill any containers regularly. Ponds are less than ideal since they often become stagnant.

Adequate shelter should be available; even if your horse or pony is to be kept partially stabled, there will be occasions when he will be glad of it. Such shelter could be provided by a building, or by natural features such as a line of trees. The grass itself should be neither overlush, nor should it be so poor as to be totally lacking in nutritional value. Good pasture consists of timothy, brome, orchard grass, clover, Bermuda grass, bluegrass, or preferably a mixture of this types. Avoid pasture that has poisonous plants growing in it, since many of these are a sign of poor quality grazing, and all are dangerous and will need complete eradication before a pony can safely be allowed to graze.

You may feel more wary keeping your pony in certain areas. Near towns, and where footpaths cross the field, there may be the danger of animals being teased, or even maliciously let out. Security is important in such cases, and it is worth freezemarking all the animals, and putting a stout padlock and chain on both sides of the gate so that it can neither be opened nor lifted off its hinges. The field itself and the perimeters should also be regularly checked in case rubbish has been thoughtlessly thrown in, or fencing damaged.

Q. What sort of plants are dangerous to my pony? And how should I get rid of such poisonous plants?

A. Poisonous plants can be a real problem, and you should keep a careful eye out for them; even if your field is apparently clear when you first check it, seeds can still be carried by the wind, and plants may start to grow later. While flora tends to be regional, among the most common poisonous plants are: castor beans, hemlock, locoweed, vetch, laurel, rhododendron, juniper, Japanese yew, bracken fern, horsetail, death camas, nightshade, red maple leaves, chokecherries, oleander, yellow star thistle, and wild tobacco. Some of these plants may also be more palatable dead than alive, and so should always be removed from the field and burned if they have been pulled or sprayed, or the animals removed until the plants are completely desiccated.

Hay should always be shaken out before feeding, as it can sometimes contain poisonous plants if it comes from poor quality pasture which, if not noticed, may be ingested with fatal results. Pulling by hand is easiest when the ground is slightly wet, but often fails to remove the roots completely, and is in any case time-consuming. Poisonous plants and weeds can be eliminated by being dug or burned out, or eradicated with herbicide. Your local county extension agent can advise you on the most suitable product to use, and provide a more complete list of poisonous plants.

Q. There are a lot of weeds in my field that seem to be taking over and stifling the grass. What is the best way of removing them?

A. Weeds are commonly a sign of badly drained or infertile soil, and the best way of eradicating them is to deal with these two problems, as well as by spraying. If drainage is poor (sometimes so bad that pools of water can be seen sitting on the surface), the air pockets in the soil become filled with moisture, starving the grass roots of oxygen and thus arresting development. This sort of soil is also cold. You may need to seek expert advice and have a survey done properly so that a system with correct spacing and fill material is set up which is suitable for the type of soil. Check first for yourself that the problem does not lie in blocked-up existing drainage ditches and outlets. If you need further advice, you could consult your local county extension agent.

Before fertilizing a field, you should first have a soil analysis performed; this needs to be done every four to five years. This will be provided on request by your county extension agent or the state department of agriculture, and they will be able to tell you what is required. It is no good just adding things willy-nilly or you

PERENNIAL
RYEGRASS

TIMOTHY

COCKSFOOT

MEADOW
FESCUE

SHEEPS
FESCUE

BENT
GRASS

YARROW

CLOVER

BURNET

CHICORY

DANDELION

Fig. 15. Types of grasses and herbs.

OAK   YEW   PRIVET   RAGWORT

COWBANE   DEADLY   WATER   ACONITE
             NIGHTSHADE   DROPWORT

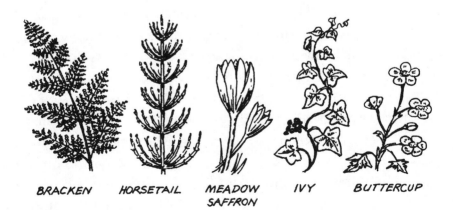

BRACKEN   HORSETAIL   MEADOW   IVY   BUTTERCUP
                      SAFFRON

Fig. 16. Poisonous plants.

could upset the balance of nutrients already present. It is worth a little effort to improve your pasture; remember that the quality of grass is only going to be as good as the soil beneath it, and good grass can provide a large proportion of your horse or pony's diet.

Q. My field is in such a terrible state that I am wondering whether it is worth plowing it up and reseeding it?

A. Such a task is very much a last resort, and not really one to be undertaken by the amateur; you will need assistance from a local farmer or county extension agent. You will also be unable to use the land for horses to graze for several months, and it will be unsuitable in any case for some time for youngsters. You should find though, that correct grazing management, fertilizing, and harrowing or plowing can improve a pasture considerably over just a few years.

Q. What sort of maintenance does my field require?

A. If you do not actually own the grazing land but lease it, first check to find out who is responsible for any maintenance, and to what degree. However good your intentions may be, you cannot simply trample on the toes of the owner of the land—or at least not without asking permission first. As far as maintenance is concerned, a soil analysis should be performed every four to five years, and fertilizers then added as required. Small areas especially need careful management, and will need to be rested occasionally. Larger areas of land often benefit from being divided into smaller ones which can be grazed in rotation, so giving the grass a chance to recover. The horses should be moved on when the grass is short—but not bare. Bare grazing land will burn up easily in the summer heat, encourage weeds, and take a long time to recover.

Fig. 17. Harrowing.

Reintroduce the horses to the pasture again when the grass is about 4 to 5 inches long. If it is longer it begins to lose its nutritional value, and there will be waste as much of it will be trampled down. Cattle grazing in rotation with horses is beneficial, if the former are allowed to follow through afterward. They are less selective grazers, and will eat coarser grass left by horses and help to break the worm cycle, since they are not natural hosts of the same parasites. If grazing with cattle is not practical, the ranker patches of grass can be mown to allow room for younger, sweeter shoots to grow without being stifled. In small areas, you can pick up the droppings on a daily basis. If left longer than this, the surrounding grass will become sour and the area ignored.

It is also worth harrowing or plowing your pasture each spring in late February/March, as it will remove moss and dead grass left after the winter. If fertilizing afterward, it also helps to open the ground up a bit more, making it easier for the fertilizer to be absorbed more quickly. Either a neighboring farmer or someone else with whom you've arranged to do the plowing will be able to do this job; the only implement that will be of any use is a heavy spiked chain or springtooth-type harrow.

Q. If my horse is grazing a large field, is it still necessary to worm him as often as I would if he was on a smaller field?

A. Regular worming is very important. Although it is impossible to get rid of them completely, they must be controlled if the animal is to remain in good health. For this reason, paddocks must be properly managed, and all the animals wormed every six to eight weeks. They should also be wormed all at the same time if it is to be effective; otherwise, one will continually be ingesting the eggs from the others. Change the wormer used frequently, as a degree of immunity can be built up. Do not just change brands, but look to see what the anthelmintic is, and change that. Ask your vet for advice on a worming schedule appropriate for your circumstances.

Q. What is the best type of fencing to have?

A. Post-and-rail or post-and-board fencing looks striking and is perhaps the ideal fencing, but can be expensive, requiring a minimum of three rails to make an imposing fence. Other types of fencing include electric rope or tape fencing (which gives the horse an uncomfortable warning jolt when he leans against it); steel pipe or PVC (polyvinylchloride) panels; and coated high-tensile wire. Sometimes the types are combined, as in a wooden fence with an electric wire across the top. Much depends on the pasture to be enclosed and the number and type of horses (e.g., a stallion might need a stronger enclosure if mares are nearby).

If they are in good repair, stone walls can provide adequate fencing for horses. These walls should be regularly checked as to their condition, and any fallen stones picked up and replaced. Stone walls will usually have electric fencing across the top; otherwise, horses might paw the stones away and jump over and escape.

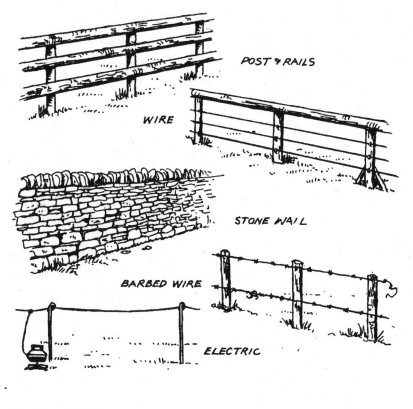

Fig. 18. Types of fencing.

Barbed wire isn't the best fencing choice, as horrific accidents can result from horses becoming caught in it; it also tends to pull the mane out when they reach underneath it. If you have no other choice (for example, if you have to share your grazing with cattle) then you will simply have to ensure that the strands are always kept taut, and a pair of wire cutters should be kept nearby in case of an emergency.

Electric fencing is not always reliable as a form of permanent fencing, but it can be a useful way of dividing a pasture in order either to rest it, or to allow it to grow for hay. It is easy to set up, and to move around as required. It needs checking quite frequently to ensure that the current running through the wire is not being shorted out by tall weeds or anything else. Horses or ponies unused to electric fencing should be led up to it and around the boundary before allowing them loose, so that they have some respect for it, and an idea of the location. Strips of colored plastic hung on the wire, or one of the types of electric fencing designed with horses in mind, will be more clearly visible.

Q. My pony is really bad about being caught, which is very annoying, particularly when I want to get somewhere for a certain time.

A. This is a habit which will take some time to cure. You may be able to catch him on occasion by cornering him, but this obviously requires quite a few people, is impractical when you are on your own, and will not make him any easier to catch. If you are to eventually be able to catch him unaided whenever you want to, then he must come to associate it with something pleasant. This means that a long-term view needs to be taken, and although at first there may be days when you cannot get near him, there will be others when he is fine, and these occasions will increase.

Try to catch him at least once a day; when you are successful, bring him in and give him a small feed. Do not catch him just to ride him, or he will continue to be wary. Make a fuss over him, give him a quick brush over and check his feet, and then turn him out again. He will begin to look forward to your visits when he knows that there will be a treat for him, and it does not always involve working. Leave a snug-fitting halter on him with a short length of rope attached to it, as this will make it easier for you to catch him. When the grass improves in the summer, you may find that he reverts to his old ways; if it is impossible to catch him on your own, you may have to consider using hobbles, or moving him to a barer piece of pasture and supplying him with extra supplementary feed instead.

Q. My pony keeps jumping out of his field, and I am worried that he will either injure himself one day doing so, or be hurt while he is out. How can I keep him in?

A. Unless he is on a diet, first make sure that he is not hungry and simply going in search of more food. Some horses and ponies do seem to enjoy the challenge of escaping from their surroundings, though, in which case you will have to either make the fence so high that he is unable to jump it, or hobble him. If he lives on his own, advertising to share your pasture with another pony, or buying him a companion, might encourage him to stay put.

6

Stabling, Bedding, and Stable Equipment

Q. How can I stop my pony from kicking over his water bucket? He keeps doing it, and so is always very thirsty the next morning when he has no water left.

A. This can be a really annoying habit, as well as an expensive one, since the bedding inevitably becomes soaked through and has to be thrown out. There are several solutions. You could, for example, install an automatic watering system, although this will need to be well insulated to prevent it from freezing up in the winter months. They are quite expensive, however, and if he starts to play with the water, can end up leaving the bed just as wet. You could alternatively place his water bucket in the center of a tire, or else buy a plastic garbage can to use as a water container. These are easy to clean out and once filled are so heavy that they cannot be knocked over. There are also a variety of pails which can be hung up against the walls of the stall.

Q. My horse has started nipping people over the stable door—I think that a lot of this is due to people giving him treats. I am sure that he will really hurt someone one day, but it seems to be a difficult habit to correct (even though I do discipline him if he tries to nip).

A. Feeding treats quickly leads to horses and ponies becoming bad-tempered if an expected tidbit is withheld. For this reason, put a notice up outside his stall, requesting that treats are not given since they make him irritable, and explain it clearly to anyone you catch ignoring the sign. Since he has already started nipping, you will have to either muzzle him or put a grill up on his stable door, so that he cannot actually grab people as they walk past.

Q. I am going to build a stable soon, but what size should it be?

A. The size of your horse or pony will determine the size of stable that you want. Too small a stall will discourage him from lying down, while too big an area may encourage him to roll, which could result in him becoming "cast" (his feet getting trapped against the wall so that he is unable to rise). The following interior dimensions would be about right:

14.2hh and under	10' × 12' (approximately)
14.2hh-15.2hh	12' × 12' (approximately)
over 15.2hh	12' × 14' (approximately)

Q. My pony keeps barging out of his stable every time I open the door—I just don't seem to be able to stop him from getting past me.

A. This is a case of bad manners; your pony obviously does not have much respect for your authority. Try to be a little more positive when handling him generally, so that he feels less inclined to push his luck. You will need to be very careful in the way in which you enter his stall, too. If there are two bolts on the bottom door, always undo the bottom bolt first—if you leave it until last and he rushes out, you could get a nasty bang on the head. If the stable opens into a yard, close all the gates before attempting to enter anyway. Do not invite trouble by throwing the door wide open, or leaving your pony untied while mucking out. Only open the door as wide as is necessary for you to get inside until you can get a halter on and tie him up. Once inside, never leave the door ajar, but bolt it securely behind you. Not only do you need to be quick about getting inside, but if necessary be ready to give him a good smack if he tries to push you aside. When you have time, make a minor adjustment to the stable by adding a breast bar, which can be slid through a bracket set on either side of the doorway on the inside. This should be of fairly solid wood, and can be left in place at all times, except when you are actually leading him in and out of the stable. This is also a pleasant way in the summer of keeping the stable cooler, since the bottom door can be left open.

Fig. 19. A breast bar.

Q. My horse has started kicking his stable door, and is driving everyone crazy with the noise. What can be done about it?

A. Part of this behavior could be caused by boredom—so make sure that he is turned out as much as possible. If you are able to, swap stables with someone, so that he is also positioned in a part of the yard where there is plenty to look at. Provide him with a haynet with smaller holes, so that it takes him longer to eat up his hay, and perhaps give him a swinging ball or another horse toy to keep him occupied. He may behave worse at certain times (such as feeding time) if he gets impatient, so have everything ready rather than making him wait. Some horses do begin to enjoy the sound they make after a while, and whatever diversions you provide, it can be difficult to get this type to stop. Pad the interior with old carpeting or rubber matting as this will both deaden the sound and protect his legs.

Q. My mare is very head-shy, and is nervous about going into her stable even though the doorway is both wide and high. It is getting very time-consuming to persuade her to go in, and sometimes we have to give up and leave her out. I am reluctant to use force; we tried smacking her once, but she got so worked up she became almost impossible. Are there any other, less time-consuming ways of getting her in, other than by bribery?

A. You might try putting a towel or jacket over her head so that she cannot see where she is going, and reversing her into the stable—you will need to be very careful that she does not bang her hips on the door frame. If this does not work, you will have to go back to bribery and coaxing, or else resign yourself to keeping her out all year round. If you become really stuck, a field shelter which can have a couple of slip rails put across the entrance may

Fig. 20. Reversing into a stable.

be the only other solution for giving her some extra shelter in the winter.

Q. I keep my pony out all year round, but as he is very attached to the other pony he lives with, and jumps out of the field if left on his own, I have to stable him for a few hours occasionally. The trouble is, he tries to climb out over the bottom door; if I close the top one he just kicks and kicks at the walls. How can I keep him in if I can't close the top door?

A. He is probably annoyed at not being able to see out, or perhaps a bit claustrophobic. Fit a grill instead—he will still be able to see out, but not get out. Alternatively, cut an oval-shaped hole in the top door, and then close it; he will still be able to put his head through the hole, but he won't be able to squeeze himself through.

Fig. 21. A hole in the stable door to prevent escape and weaving.

Q. My horse has learned how to undo the top bolt of his stable door and let himself out—how can I stop him before he escapes onto a road?

A. Putting a lead-rope clip onto the bolt as many people do is not really the answer, as these can still be undone, and can get caught on a lip. Make sure there is a bottom bolt—a kick bolt is best—and invest in a "horse-proof" bolt for the top one. This has a plate incorporated into it which makes it impossible for anyone other than a human to open it. Do not be tempted to padlock him in, as this could be very dangerous in the event of a fire.

Q. My horse paws at the ground just in front of the stable door. This is beginning to make a dent in the concrete, and wears the toes on his front shoes very quickly. Is there any way of making him stop?

A. Boredom often accounts for many of these habits, so try to give him as much as possible to keep his mind occupied. Put a rubber mat down just in front of the stable door, as this will deaden the

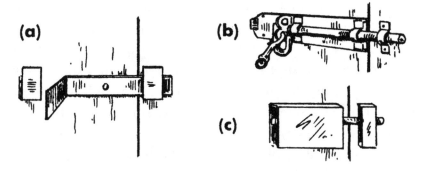

Fig. 22. Door bolts:
(a) A kick bolt operated by foot, suitable as a bottom bolt.
(b) A trigger clip to prevent the horse from drawing a bolt back.
(c) An enclosed horse-proof bolt.

sound, and save a lot of wear and tear on his shoes. You can find heavy mats of this type advertised in horse magazines.

Q. My horse is always eating her bedding, and gets very fat because of this. Even if I put her fresh straw in last thing at night, she has eaten most of it by next morning, and is standing on exposed concrete. I can't afford to keep on using straw at this rate, and she is so fat I am almost ashamed of her.

A. Being overweight is bad for all horses and ponies, and while stabling for part of the day is one way of restricting the food intake, it is not going to be a great success unless you can stop her from eating her bedding. See if you can find a small, bare paddock, or even a cattle yard where she can wander around; it is more natural than standing in a stable for hours on end, and she may be happier and less inclined to pick at her bedding when she is stabled again.

If there is no alternative but to keep her stabled, or she is so greedy that nothing is going to stop her from wolfing it down, you will need to find ways of discouraging her. Straw eaten in large quantities can irritate the gut or cause a blockage. If she lies down on insufficient bedding she could easily injure herself, and might become reluctant to urinate, leading to kidney complaints. Try changing her bedding to sawdust, shavings, or newspaper, which are less tempting. If she continues trying to nibble at these, it could prove just as dangerous in the long run, and the bed should be lightly sprinkled with a diluted non-toxic disinfectant which will give it a slightly unpleasant taste. Fresh bedding should always be well mixed in with the older, slightly soiled bedding for the same reason. Should these measures prove ineffective, you will have no choice but to muzzle her.

Q. My manure pile seems to be permanently out of control. It spreads all over the place—is there some method of keeping it tidy?

A. It helps to keep it in place if you build three retaining walls from concrete blocks, which then only leaves you one side to keep tidy. Turn it over regularly and mix in straw, shavings, and leaf matter; this will help it generate more heat so that it rots down quicker. The heat will also help to destroy any worm eggs in the droppings. The other alternative is to do away with a manure pile altogether, and muck out directly into plastic sacks. These can then be placed in a tidy pile, the tops tied with string, ready to sell or give away to neighbors for their gardens.

Q. My horse has started chewing the wood in his stable; how can I stop him?

A. Cover the areas with anti-cribbing spray, hot pepper, or another unpalatable but nontoxic substance; although messy, it will stop him. He may be chewing because of a lack in his diet, so add a mineral and vitamin supplement to his feed each day.

Q. I have noticed that my horse often stands at his stable door, swaying from side to side. What is this called, and why does he do it?

A. This habit is known as "weaving," and is usually the result of boredom, often combined with a high-strung temperament. Try to achieve a regular routine so that your horse does not become over-anxious, and turn him out as often as possible, so that he is less likely to get bored. Weaving can lead to a loss of condition, poor digestion, and damage the legs and feet, so you should do all you can to prevent it. Do keep him stabled away from other horses if possible, and away from youngsters, as they often tend to imitate. Fit some kind of anti-weaving grid to his door; preferably the sort which allows him to look out, although not to weave. A full grid which stops him from putting his head over the bottom door will often encourage him to start weaving at the back of the box, rather than to break the habit. Or cut a hole in the upper door to alleviate boredom. (See Fig. 21, pg 74.)

Q. Sometimes my horse takes hold of his stable door with his top teeth, and I notice him swallowing and making an odd sound. Is he in pain, or is this a normal thing?

A. Give him plenty to keep him occupied; like most stable vices, "cribbing," as it is called, is often due to boredom. Once the habit is established, it is quite difficult to break, and it is not unknown for a horse turned out in a field to stand cribbing on the fence rather than grazing. It can also lead to "windsucking" which is when the animal learns how to swallow air without having to hold onto anything, and so just applying an anti-cribbing spray to projecting surfaces is not enough. You will need to put a crib strap of some kind on; the type made with a shape aluminum hinge is usually most successful. This prevents him from arching his neck and

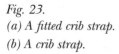

Fig. 23.
(a) A fitted crib strap.
(b) A crib strap.

swallowing air in the manner you describe. Swallowing air like this can lead to colic and to poor digestion, so it is worth taking some preventive measures.

7

Feeding

Q. Is it really necessary to feed a supplement—surely horses and ponies get all the minerals and vitamins they require from their diets?

A. Feeding a supplement is a way of ensuring that a horse or pony receives all the nutrients he needs. Mineral salts are vital to the biological processes that take place in the body, and are continually being lost through sweating, and in the urine and droppings. In the wild they would normally be replaced since the horse would have access to unlimited areas; but since most domesticated animals are restricted to comparatively small areas of grazing, or are stabled, these minerals and vitamins need to be artificially added to the diet. Often the normal diet is not entirely sufficient to meet the horse's needs, since modern agricultural methods have produced hay and grains that contain lower levels of these nutrients than in the past. Deficiencies can build up over a number of years, and can result in more serious effects; symptoms of deficiencies include when the animal is seen to start stripping bark off trees, eating the soil, or even his own droppings. He is simply trying to find a supply of the nutrients he is lacking.

When feeding a supplement, it is by far the easiest to choose one that is already balanced and prepared for your horse and the type of work which he is going to be doing; if you are unsure which type of supplement is most suitable, the manufacturers should be able to give you some advice. Some of the "complete" feeds, such as coarse mixes and cubes, already contain amounts of vitamins and minerals, so if you are feeding these in some proportion, the amount of supplement given will need to be adjusted accordingly. Once again, if you are unsure as to how much should be given to make up a fully balanced diet, then you should consult the manufacturer—most are very helpful.

The other alternative to actually adding a measured amount of supplement to the diet is to provide a lick of some kind to which the horse can help himself. This can be left in the feed manger, or hung up in the stable or field. Keep an eye on your horse when using it, however, as some horses tend to just crunch their way through. In that case, it would be wisest to return to adding supplement to the feeds, or else removing the lick for part of the day. Too much is as bad as too little—and unnecessarily expensive.

Q. I have been told that I should add some salt to my horse's feed each day—yet I have also heard that eating salt is harmful to humans. Surely the same applies to horses as well?

A. Often it is not the type of food eaten by humans which is detrimental to the health, simply the quantity of it. Over-indulgence of anything is bound to be harmful eventually. A small amount of salt added to the daily diet is not going to do much harm when considering the size and bulk of a horse as compared to a human—and it does have its benefits. It is important in the digestive processes, helps to replace salt lost through sweating (sweat is far more concentrated in horses than in humans), and creates a less acidic environment in the stomach, thereby making it less hospitable to worms. When feeding a diet high in oats, it also helps to combat the decalcifying effect they have. Provide a salt block, or a mineral block—which contains trace elements—in a salt lick holder to keep it off the floor and your horse will be able to help himself to what he needs.

Q. My horse eats his feeds really quickly and I am sure this doesn't do him any good. How can I make him eat more slowly?

A. He will not get as much benefit from his feed if he is not chewing them properly; the gastric juices will not be able to work on them as easily, and he may get colic. Do not feed him in a situation where he feels he has to gobble his feed quickly before someone else takes it away from him; if possible, feed him well away from other horses and ponies likely to chase him off (he will still feel this even if you are near him), and preferably where he has peace and quiet on his own. Break up a salt block into large pieces, which can be left in his feed bowl—it will help to slow him down, and this type of salt is so hard that he will not be able to crunch his way through it.

Q. My husband saves grass clippings from the lawn for my horse, but a friend told me this could be dangerous—is this true?

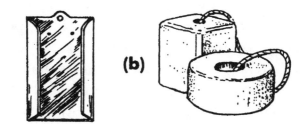

Fig. 24.
(a) A salt lick holder.
(b) Salt licks threaded with rope.

A. Grass clippings are best disposed of by making them into a compost heap at the bottom of your garden rather than feeding them to your horse. They could easily choke him, or pack down into a solid mass in the stomach, causing a blockage of the gut. In this state they are likely to ferment, and the gases given off by this process might cause a fatal rupture. Added to this, they could well prove toxic if oil has dripped onto them from the mower, or if poisonous plants have been picked up, or a lawn treatment used.

Q. How much should I feed my horse?

A. This depends upon several factors, including size of the horse and its level of activity. You should work out your horse's weight (height is not a good guide as to weight, since build varies so much). You can do this by either using a special tape measure available from most tack shops, or for a more accurate guide, by having him weighed on a large-animal scale, if one is available. Alternatively, you might try working out the following equation, although it will give you only a rough estimate:

$$\frac{girth^2 \text{ (in inches)} \times \text{length between pt. of shoulder and pt. of buttock (in inches)}}{290}$$

This will give you an approximate weight in pounds on which to base your calculations. Generally speaking, you should feed 2 pounds for every 100 pounds body weight, although horses in very hard work may need slightly more than this, while ponies, or animals of certain breeding, may be very thrifty and require rather less. How much of this amount you then divide up into a pellet ration, and how much is fed as roughage and forage (hay and grazing) depends upon the type of work done. If that diet turns the horse into one that's more energetic than you want him to be, you'd cut back on his grain and increase his hay (except for alfalfa, which has lots of protein; hay is the equivalent of mashed potatoes—bulk and some energy, but less than oats or corn).

As a rough guide, try to work it out along the following lines:

	Pellets	*Roughage, forage*
light work	25%	75%
medium work	50%	50%
heavy work	75%	25%

The amount of bulk received should never drop beneath 25 percent of the total ration, since it is essential in keeping the digestive system working correctly. It is also important to observe the horse's condition carefully; if he becomes overweight or appears too lean, the diet should be adjusted accordingly, both in proportion and content.

To a large extent, good feeding depends upon the owner's observation, judgment, and "feel" for the situation, together with a little trial and error, until the right formula for the individual animal has been found. You should also feel free to consult with your vet to make sure that your horse is receiving an adequate and suitable diet.

Q. My horse seems to eat his hay very quickly. As he tends to get fat very easily, I have to keep him stabled quite a lot, and cannot give him much to eat—yet once he has finished his hay he must get very bored.

A. The solution to this problem is to put the hay in a net which has smaller holes. Make sure that it is securely fixed, however, since if it is pulled down during the night he could injure himself badly if he got tangled up in it. It should also be fastened high enough up to prevent him from getting a foot caught in it. You might also provide him with a swinging ball or similar toy that will keep him amused once he has finished eating.

Q. My horse is really difficult to keep weight on, which isn't helped by the fact that he is also a fussy feeder. What can I do about this?

A. Just as some people are able to eat as much cake and chocolate as they like and never put on any weight, so can some horses eat large quantities without becoming overweight. This can be very worrying for the owner, however. Do check that he is regularly wormed, and that his teeth are not sharp, as both of these could contribute to the lack of condition. It might also be a wise precaution to ask the vet to give him a blood test to ensure that there is no other reason; he could take a sample of droppings at the same time for a worm count. Consider the diet itself, as well; it should be of the highest quality. Your horse should have hay on demand whenever stabled, and peace and quiet in which to eat and digest each feed. Small feedings often are better than one or two large ones; not only will digestion be more thorough, but it is less discouraging to the fussy feeder. There are also plenty of things you can add to the feed, both to make it more tempting and to help put some weight on.

Sugar beet pulp: This can be bought in either pulp or cube form; the former must be soaked for at least 12 hours, or until it will absorb no more water, while cubes, being more compact, require around 24 hours. It is highly dangerous if fed unsoaked, since it will swell in the gut and cause a blockage. Soak in plenty of water, since it will absorb around three times its own volume. Although it is the dried and crushed remains of sugar beet once the sugar has been extracted, it still contains quite a high proportion of sugar, which makes it very palatable. A maximum of 6 pounds (soaked weight) may be fed each day, but in practice, around 2 pounds is usually sufficient, due to its slightly laxative nature. Overfeeding can lead to scouring, but experience will show how much each individual can take. Care must be exercised in its preparation during the summer, when the heat is likely to make it ferment, thereby unsafe to feed.

Carrots: Sliced lengthwise (not across, which can lead to choking) and added to the feed; these can encourage a fussy feeder to eat up.

Molasses: Molasses can be added to sweeten a feed, or make a mash more tempting, and is fairly safe to feed. It should be diluted first in order to mix it in; 1 part molasses to 5 parts water. Along the same lines, honey can be used instead, but is more expensive to purchase.

Eggs: One or two of these can be added to the feed, and will also help to put a bloom on the coat.

Q. I am about to buy a horse, but am unsure about what I should feed it. Lots of my friends mix up their own feeds and have offered advice, while several others recommended that I buy a complete feed. Which is best?

A. Many people like to make up their own mixture of different types of grains, since it can be easily adjusted to specific requirements, and everything that has gone into it is known. However, those with limited time or storage space often prefer complete feeds—coarse mixes, cubes, and so forth, which have been specially mixed at the factory so as to provide an instant, balanced diet, without the need to add anything else other than hay. If you choose the latter method, you should make sure that you choose the right type of feed to suit your horse and the type of work it is expected to do; if in any doubt, either the manufacturer or feed dealer should be able to advise you. For the one-horse owner, sometimes this can prove to be the cheapest method of feeding, as well as the handiest, since there is likely to be less danger of the feed going bad before it can be used up. In any event, you ought to check with the previous owner, and find out what the horse is used to receiving; there may be certain types of feed which do not suit him for some reason, and it will enable you to avoid upsetting his system by making any sudden changes.

If you wish to change to a different system of feeding, or to introduce a different feed, try to make substitutions as gradually as possible, over a period of weeks, otherwise colic can occur. When opting to mix up your own feeds from different grains, it helps if you know something about each before deciding upon the quantities you will use.

Here are a few brief guidelines:

Oats: Probably the best balanced of all the grains as they contain the correct proportion of protein, carbohydrates, and fats. They should be fed crushed or bruised, rather than whole, for better digestion. They can prove to be rather "heating" for some animals—that is to say, they may make some horses and ponies over-excitable and difficult to handle.

Corn: This is a very high-energy feed, and can lead to laminitis if fed in quantity, especially in ponies. Only small quantities should be given (a maximum of 2 pounds) and it should be introduced very gradually to the diet. It is normally bought whole or cracked.

Bran: This is used as a filler to add bulk to the feed, or it can be fed as a laxative in the form of a mash the evening before a rest day. It should be bought as processed bran, and preferably not fed to young stock as it can have adverse effects on bone growth. Never feed it dry, as it can cause choking.

Q. How do I make a bran mash?

A. Place 3 to 4 pounds of bran in the bottom of a bucket, add a good handful of salt, and 3 pints of boiling water. Stir thoroughly with a stick, so that it becomes a crumbly mixture, and cover with a piece of old cloth or towel and leave to stand for half an hour. Check the temperature before feeding, as bran holds the heat well, and it may be a bit hot.

Q. I understand that bad feeding can cause colic—what sort of things does this include?

A. A number of things can cause colic, but bad stable management and feeding are the most frequent factors. This includes:

- Working too soon after a feed—at least one hour should be left after the feed has been eaten before commencing exercise. This is because the greatest muscular strain takes place during this first hour; during the second the gastric juices get to work before the food passes into the gut from the stomach.
- Over-rich grass—or if the horse is unaccustomed to grazing; changes in routine must be made slowly.
- Sudden changes of diet
- Poor quality feed
- Bolting feed
- Poisonous plants
- Feeding a hot horse, or watering a hot horse
- Irregular feeding
- Drinking after feeding—many horses will sip at their water while eating their feed, and this in itself does not normally cause problems. However, if the horse takes a long drink

after the feed, it will wash the feed out of the stomach and into the gut, causing poor digestion and possible colic.

- Too much feed at once—no feed should be larger than 4 pounds in weight as the stomach is comparatively small in horses and cannot cope with more.
- Giving hay after a feed—this will push the feed through the stomach, and it may block the gut.
- Other causes of colic are: worms, sharp teeth—which interferes with proper mastication—windsucking, cribbing, eating bedding, sand in the stomach, stagnant water, stones in the kidneys, and infection in the alimentary canal.

Grooming and Clipping

8

Q. My horse's tail is very wispy and thin, so that it never looks attractive at shows—it has been like this ever since I bought him nearly two years ago. Is there anything I can do to improve its appearance?

A. Not all horses are blessed with thick, luxuriant tails and a wispy one can sometimes look pretty awful, as well as being much less effective as a flyswatter during the summer months. The best thing to do is to stop using a brush on it at all, and to just tease the tangles out very carefully with your fingers so that the hairs aren't broken off. Only use a brush when preparing for a show, making sure that the tail is clean first, and then using only a very soft brush. Put a little baby oil on the brush before use, as this will help to prevent it from pulling at the hairs, and will keep the tail more tangle-free in the future. It sometimes helps if you use a conditioner for dry hair after shampooing it, as this type of tail is usually rather brittle. To improve the appearance further when showing, divide the tail into three sections while it is still damp after washing, and braid down its length, securing the end with an elastic band. When the tail is dry, this will give it a slightly wavy appearance, making it look much fuller than it really is, particularly if the end is also trimmed off level.

89

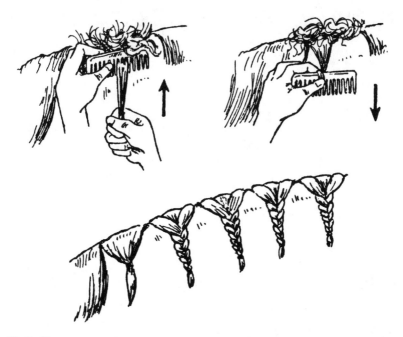

Fig. 25. Pulling mane and stable braids.

Q. I'm having problems with my horse's mane; it is really thick, and although I've tried laying it over with a damp water brush, it doesn't seem to make much difference—it still sticks up in the air!

A. Some manes do grow very thickly, especially in horses or ponies with a certain amount of coarser breeds, or those who have previously been sheared. Keep the mane properly pulled first of all, removing a few hairs at a time from the underside, aiming not just at shortening it, but thinning it out too. Don't attempt to do too much all at once, either, or your horse is likely to get sore, and will rub, making the situation even worse. Then lay the mane over with a damp water brush, and put in some loose stable braids, securing the ends with elastic bands. These can be left in for one or two days, and will help to train the mane to stay on one side rather than sticking up. Always dampen the mane down each time you groom anyway, and pop the braids back in when the mane starts to get rebellious again.

Q. However many times I wash it, my gray gelding's tail still has a yellowish tinge. How can I make it look white again?

A. When shampooing the tail, use a good mane and tail shampoo. Be careful to use it only on the hairs of the tail, however, and not on the dock, in case it irritates the skin and makes him rub. Use a conditioner afterwards, and when giving the final rinse, add a bluing rinse (or any other product designed to enhance a horse's mane and tail) to the water; this will give a really dazzling blue-white finish. These products are available from most supermarkets at minimal expense. Finally, once the tail is dry, put some baby oil onto a body brush and go through the tail thoroughly with it. The baby oil will coat the hairs, and help to stop them from getting so dirty again.

Q. I am having a lot of trouble picking up my two-year-old pony's feet. Not only is it difficult to get him to pick each one up, but once he has, he inevitably slams it back down again before I am ready.

A. You will find it easier to pick up his feet if you first make sure he is standing squarely, so that he is better able to balance himself. Slide a hand down the inside of the leg that you wish him to pick up, and when you reach the fetlock joint, grasp it firmly, and either click to him or give the command "Up!" Should he resist, lean gently against him with your shoulder, so that he is encouraged to take his weight off that particular foot, and pinch the base of the tendon, just above the fetlock joint, between thumb and forefinger as well. Do remember that youngsters tend to be rather uncoordinated, and he may find it difficult to lift his feet up very high, or to keep his balance on three legs for very long, so make sure that you are not being overly demanding in this respect. If he is not genuinely losing his balance, and is persisting in this habit out of sheer stubbornness, you must put your own foot down firmly, and reprimand him sharply, accompanied by a smack if necessary.

Q. I thought I'd pull my pony's mane the other day as it is getting very long. When I started, he wasn't too badly behaved at all, but after a bit he started getting very irritable, swinging his quarters around so that he squashed me against the wall, and throwing his head about. He has been just as bad ever since—how on earth can I make him behave so that I can finish his mane off?

A. Some horses and ponies are more sensitive than others when it comes to mane and tail pulling, and if you try to do too much in one session, they will become very sore, making them bad tempered and also inclined to rub, spoiling all your efforts. Rather than doing a lot at once, just attempt a little each day, preferably after exercise. Select the longest hairs from the underside of the mane, using a trimming comb to backcomb and sepa-

Fig. 26.
(a) A homemade twitch.
(b) A twitch when put on.

rate them. Wrap the hairs once around the comb, or place your thumb firmly on top of them, and pull downward so that they come out from the roots rather than breaking. Make sure that you take hold of only a few hairs at a time, pulling them out quickly and sharply rather than tugging on them, which will be painful. Tail pulling follows a similar technique; start at the top of the dock, selecting the longest hairs from the bottom and sides, and working your way downward. If he is terribly uncooperative, you may need to resort to getting someone to hold him, and put a twitch on, but it is best to persevere for a while with this more gentle approach in order to avoid creating a mental hang-up about it all.

Q. My horse will let me groom all of his head without fuss, except for his left ear. As far as I can see, there does not seem to be any real reason for this, and it is becoming quite a nuisance.

A. Since your horse does not object to the rest of his head being groomed, just one ear, it sounds likely that there is something wrong with it, and it is not just due to misbehaving. It is always best not to jump to conclusions, and if it is difficult just touching this ear, then it is unlikely that you have been able to give it a really thorough inspection. He could be suffering from an ear infection, mites, or even have a hay seed stuck in it, which would cause a lot of discomfort, and explain his behavior. The best thing to do is to call the vet and get him to check it properly, since many of these problems are not immediately visible, and it will certainly take the two of you to get a better look.

Q. I have lost confidence when grooming my mare. All she does is try and nip and occasionally kick out at me, so I end up grooming her as little as possible. Is there anything I can do to try and improve her temper? I really

dread grooming as I am sure I will get hurt one day. Otherwise she is excel-
lent to ride, so I don't really want to part with her.

A. The fear of getting hurt is often far worse than the reality, and you are allowing it to get the better of you. The longer this state of mind continues, the more likely it is that your mare will sense your lack of authority and confidence from your actions and it is likely to make her more irritable and prone to playing up. You will simply have to take a deep breath and go in and get on with it—you cannot skimp on grooming since it could affect her health eventually. Stay fairly close to her, so that should she try to kick out she will only succeed in pushing you away from her. If you stand too far away she is far more likely to inflict serious damage. Tie her up fairly short, so that she can't reach to nip or bite, and be firm, speaking sharply to her; you can tap her nose smartly as well (if necessary) if she starts to misbehave. The chances are that with a more positive attitude she will soon quit this game, but you must first take a stand and let her know that she isn't going to get away with it—or else she will never have any respect for you.

If it helps to make you feel a bit more confident, try putting a muzzle on when grooming, so you know that she cannot possibly bite you. It is not really as horrid as it sounds; a plastic bucket type is fairly cheap and obtainable from your tack shop, but make sure it fits properly as they can sometimes rub. Your tack shop will be able to advise you on the fit if you are uncertain. Take care not to aggravate the situation since mares are often more sensitive than geldings, particularly when they are in season. Do not use stiff brushes on her more ticklish spots—under the belly, between the front and back legs, and around the flanks are the areas to be most careful of. Use a soft brush instead, firmly but patiently. When dirt and sweat are caked on, you may even find it easier to wash these places with warm water, and towel them dry afterwards. Try not to be abrupt in your movements either, but talk quietly to her as you work, since you will find that it helps steady your nerves just as much as it soothes her.

Q. I enter one or two local showing classes whenever there is a show near us, and a lot of people have told me that I should trim my horse's whiskers for these. Is this cruel? If I do decide to trim them off, how can I do this most neatly?

A. Trimming off the whiskers can improve the appearance tremendously, making a coarse head look more refined, especially if the jawline and ears are done at the same time. The hairs on the muzzle are simply "feelers" to help the horse pick out its food when grazing. It is not cruel to cut them off, and is not at all painful, and he will manage quite easily without them; should you change your mind, they will grow back very quickly in any case. You can either trim them off very carefully using a pair of scissors, or for a quicker and neater result use a disposable ladies' safety razor instead. It is best to do this on the morning of a show so that you don't end up with a light growth of stubble. The jawline can be trimmed using scissors, as can the ears. When trimming the latter, press the edges, but do not actually remove the hairs from the inside, as they are functional in helping to prevent particles of dirt from getting inside.

Fig. 27. Holding an ear pressed together and trimming around the edge.

Q. I've got a three-year-old gelding which I hope to help break in soon. At the moment I handle him as much as possible, teaching him to stand, lead, pick up his feet, and so on. The trouble is that he has started to nip quite a lot—am I right in disciplining him or will he grow out of this when he has finished teething? He also chews everything around, including his lead rope when he is tied up, which I assume is related to this problem.

A. You must certainly discipline him for nipping, which may be partly due to teething, but is nonetheless inexcusable behavior. He must learn to respect you, and discover that he cannot get away with this or any other unsociable habits, or it could turn into an unpleasant and painful vice. Growl at him at the same time, and you will find that eventually he will understand your disapproval of his actions without your necessarily always having to give him a tap as well. At this age you really will have to assert your authority, or you could have real problems later on if he comes to consider you merely as one of the herd, instead of the boss.

You will have to keep your grooming tools and so forth out of temptation's way in order to keep them from being chewed, and give wooden surfaces a coat of anti-cribbing spray to give them an unpleasant taste, or else your horse will develop an expensive habit impossible to break once it is established. When you need to tie him up, use a rack chain rather than a lead rope; these are made from steel, which he will not be able to chew through. It consists of a central ring with an 18-inch length of chain on either side, and terminating in a spring clip at each end. It should, however, be looped through a piece of string which will break in an emergency, rather than attached to anything fixed.

Q. I enjoy taking my horse to shows—the trouble is that he gets so dirty overnight, and is covered in stains the next morning, whether I bring him in or leave him out in the field. This means that I always have to bathe

him on the morning of the show, which means getting up very early so that
he is dry in time; this tends to take some of the shine off his coat. Is there
any way to keep him clean so that I could bathe him the day before?

A. When your horse is dry, bring him into his stable and put a
summer sheet on, which will keep most of his body clean if it is
fairly deep. Bandage his legs too, as this will help to keep them
respectable. Make sure that there is plenty of fresh clean bedding
in his stable, and muck it out as late as possible in the evening, so
that there is as little as possible to roll in. You will probably find
that there will be a few stains in the morning, but it will not take as
long to deal with these as it would to give him a complete bath. If
you find it necessary on some occasion to wash all of him, and are
worried that he has lost some of the shine on his coat, you could
buy some coat gloss from your tack shop which works quite successfully—or, if you forget to buy it, a little furniture polish from
an aerosol can on a stable rag will also do the trick. (A small test
patch should be done first to make sure that there is no allergic
reaction, eczema, or itchiness.)

Q. A lot of books mention that you should wash your horse's sheath regu-
larly—but none of them say how to go about this.

A. Washing the sheath regularly is an important part of grooming, as dirt and dried excreta can accumulate inside, making it
both uncomfortable and allowing for the possibility of infection.
Once a week, using warm water, mild soap, and a sponge, wash out
inside the sheath as far as you can get, rinsing well with clean
water afterwards. Keep a separate sponge for this task, rather than
using the ones kept for wiping the eyes and dock. Finish off by drying with a clean towel as thoroughly as you are able to, and apply a
little petroleum jelly or baby oil to prevent any soreness. Be care-

ful of sharp fingernails and avoid wearing rings; you should be cautious when dealing with this area, anyway, as some animals are very ticklish.

Just as important a piece of hygiene is to remember to wipe beneath the dock—this again should be lightly oiled with petroleum jelly or baby oil afterwards to keep it feeling comfortable. Mares should have their udders and vulvas washed just as frequently as a gelding's sheath, if not more so, since they tend to get dirtier.

Q. I am thinking of getting my horse freezemarked, and wonder if this is likely to affect a judge's opinion when I am showing him. Also, is it at all painful?

A. Freezemarking is an excellent way of deterring thieves and well worth spending the money on. It is almost completely painless: the area marked (usually beneath the mane or saddle) will be slightly swollen for a few days, but you should be able to ride again after a week. The "branding" process destroys the pigmentation of the hair cells. When new hair starts to grow through again after about twelve weeks, it is white in color, so that the numbers and letters are visible in contrast against the coat. It is possible to freezemark gray or white animals, too: the marking irons are simply left on for a slightly longer period of time so that the hair is killed completely and the numbers and letters appear as bald patches instead. It should not affect a judge's decision in the show ring, but if you are worried, another option is to have an invisible microchip inserted in the crest of the neck by your vet.

Q. My horse is really bad about being tied up—he seems to hang back all the time and breaks quite a number of lead ropes. When I discipline him he only gets more uptight; so how can I stop this habit?

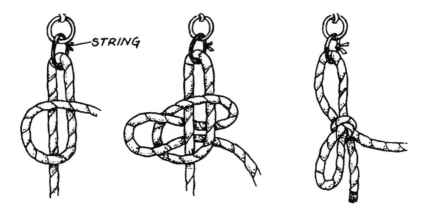

Fig. 28. Stages in the tying of a quick-release knot.

A. If he was just being naughty, some firm discipline would probably have sorted this out. It sounds more likely that your horse has perhaps had a nasty experience in the past while tied up, and obviously still panics when he feels restricted. Make sure that you do not give him any cause to hang back by being rough or abrupt while working around him. Try hanging up a small haynet to keep him occupied. Always tie him to a piece of string which will break in the event of an emergency, rather than the lead rope or his neck. Use a quick-release knot too, which can be easily undone should he become distressed, while you go to his head and reassure him. Patience will help to improve matters to a degree, but he is unlikely ever to be totally reliable about being tied up, so you should never leave him tied up on his own without supervision.

Q. My gelding has a very thick coat, even during the summer. This means that he gets terribly hot when I exercise him and he loses a lot of weight because of it. I clip him in the winter, but would it be all right to do so during the summer months as well?

A. There is no reason at all why you shouldn't—clipping him out completely sounds as if it would be the most beneficial to him, and it would mean that there would be no lines. Check him in the evenings as they are often rather cool by comparison with daytime temperatures, and he may appreciate a blanket to keep him warm.

Q. I would like to clip my horse as I think he would look much neater. What sort should I choose?

A. Clipping should be done because it is necessary to do so, not purely to improve a horse or pony's looks. The reasons for clipping are that by removing some of the thick winter coat, he will sweat less heavily and so is more likely to maintain condition, will be capable of more fast work without becoming so distressed, will be less likely to catch a chill since the coat will dry more quickly, and will be easier to keep clean. Clipping may also be necessary to make it easier to treat certain skin diseases.

However, clipping does mean that in most cases you will have to keep him warm when he is not working, by putting blankets on to replace the missing coat, and you may even have to stable him as well if you intend to clip very much off. Choose the type of clip according to how you are able to keep him, and your capabilities as a rider. Bear in mind that if he is minus rather a lot of winter coat, stabled, and not receiving a great deal of exercise, he will be a more lively ride than normal when you do take him out and he starts to feel the cold.

A *sweat clip* is quite suitable for a horse living out that does not do a great deal of work; certain types of horses often don't need a blanket, since very little hair is removed, just a strip from the throat, bottom of the neck, and chest.

If he lives outdoors, but will have to work moderately hard, you could try a fairly low *trace clip*, where hair is removed from the throat, lower part of the neck, chest, belly, and around the stifle—but a turnout blanket will be necessary, perhaps even with an extra blanket stitched inside it if the weather is very bad. The blanket

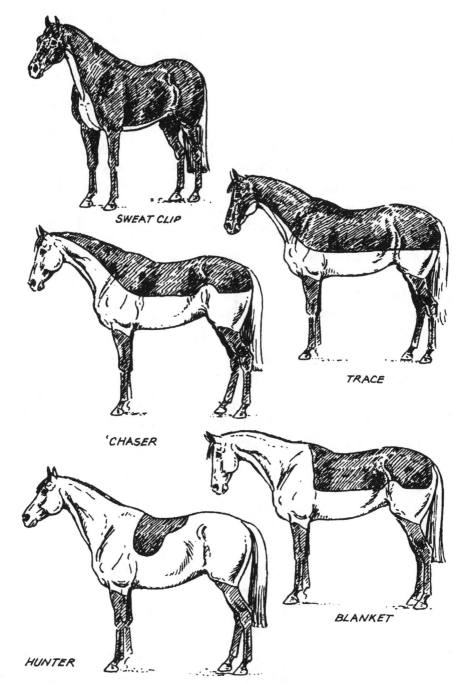

Fig. 29. Types of clips.

should be as deep as possible since the belly does get rather cold, even if only a small amount of hair has been removed.

Consider also the type of work the horse is expected to do. One which is going hunting, for example, should not have its legs clipped out, since the additional hair there will help both to keep it warm when standing still, and to give it some protection against brambles and so forth when on the move. Horses prone to feeling the cold should ideally be left with some hair covering their loins, and those tending to be "cold-backed" will also often benefit from having at least a saddle patch left on. This will also act to a degree as a cushion against soreness if the horse is going to be ridden for long periods.

Provided you are able to keep your horse stabled at nights, you can, within reason, choose a clip that will deceive the eye a little and help improve its appearance—provided, of course, that it is appropriate to all the conditions mentioned so far. A trace clip can help to make a horse with a short back look a little more proportionate, while if its legs are a little short, then a high trace clip helps to make them appear a little longer. A *blanket clip* will help shorten up a horse with a long back. A *full* or *hunter clip* is really only necessary if your horse is going to be in very hard work. Clipping the head, or a *bridle clip* (according to how much of the body hair you are removing) will also help to refine a head that looks rather coarse and hairy in the winter.

Q. My horse is really difficult to clip. I bought a set of clippers with a friend, thinking that in the long term it would work out cheaper than paying someone else to do it. I only bought my horse in the summer, and thought he would be fine about it as he was so good in every other situation. The first time I tried, though, he went berserk. I dropped the clippers, and they have just been repaired at great expense. I am now rather wary about another attempt—how can I ensure that he behaves?

A. Clipping is often the last thing on your mind if you buy a horse during the summer months, but it is always wise to inquire about such things. For the moment, persevere with a gentle approach, as he may have been frightened in the past. Run the clippers near his stall each day to try and accustom him to the noise. When he seems quite settled about this, try again, making sure that you have an assistant to hold him. You should also take the precaution of slipping your hand through the wrist loop provided on the clippers so that if he panics again you don't end up dropping them. If he still objects, try putting some cotton wool in his ears as some horses simply object to the sound.

If this makes no difference, then you may need to get your assistant to twitch him. A twitch may be made by drilling a hole in the end of a piece of sawn-off broom handle, and threading a piece of thin rope or braided baler twine approximately 24 inches in length through it, and knotting the ends securely together. This loop is then passed over the horse's top lip, and the piece of handle twisted to tighten it. On removal (which should be frequent), the nose should be rubbed vigorously to restore the circulation.

In the event that you have to resort to such measures, it is often best to just clip a little in several sessions rather than attempt to do too much and risk upsetting him even more. He may have been nicked in the past, still remember the event, and so be nervous now. Provided you don't do the same again, you can hope that he will gain in confidence with time. Make sure that the clippers themselves are not at fault. Check that they are correctly grounded so they are not giving him any little shocks, that the blades are sharp enough, and the tension correctly adjusted so they do not pull at the hairs, making the whole process unnecessarily painful.

Despite these precautions, you may still find that he is not too keen on the idea, in which case you will have to ask the vet to sedate him. You should still be careful, and restrict yourself to a reasonably small area, since these injections are not effective for very long, and the horse may start to recover full consciousness with little or no warning. Frequently, however, once the horse has been sedated and successfully clipped, it seems to accept it all much better the next time, being better behaved and not always needing sedation first.

Heads can often be a bit tricky with a nervous horse, so you might also find it a good investment to buy either a set of hand clippers or battery/rechargeable clippers of the type often used for dogs. These have smaller heads, are more maneuverable and easier to hold, and are quieter and cause less vibration.

Q. I am taking my pony to be clipped at a local riding school next week. Her previous owners have said that she is fine in this respect so I am not expecting any trouble—but are there any preparations I should make first?

A. Make sure your pony is as clean as possible, since dirt and dried sweat clogs the clippers, makes them overheat, blunts the blades, and causes them to pull painfully at the hair. Grease also makes clippers overheat, and is difficult to clip through, so try to remove the worst of it. Without actually giving him a bath you can put a capful of waterless shampoo into half a bucket of warm water, wring out a sponge in it, and then rub it vigorously against the lie of the hair. Rinse it out in the water and repeat. The grease forms a white scum on top of the water. Concentrate on the worst of the greasy areas where your pony is to be clipped, and then dry as well as possible with a towel.

Your pony should be dry when clipped, so, if you are riding over, or if he gets hot traveling in the trailer, leave some extra time and arrive early so that he can dry off. Take a halter, and also a bridle if you are not riding him over there, in case you need some extra control. If you are going to be holding him, wear rubber footwear, tie back your hair or wear a hat—this will stop your hair from getting in the way, and will certainly help to prevent you becoming covered with bits of clipped hair! Try and wear a jacket or an old shirt over your clothes too; otherwise you will find that the clippings get everywhere, and make you generally uncomfortable.

The Foot and Shoeing

9

Q. My pony is unshod at the moment, and has been since I bought him a couple of months ago. I do very little roadwork, but my friends have all told me that it is cruel to work him without shoes. Is this true?

A. If your pony has been used to working without his shoes for some time, his feet will have become quite tough and hard, in the same way as your own feet become tougher and more leathery if you spend much time barefoot. Provided that you avoid roadwork as much as possible, he should be fine, although when the ground gets very hard and dry in the summer, he may possibly get a little footsore. Otherwise, there is no reason why you should work him with shoes if you do not wish to, but do have the farrier call on a regular basis as his feet will still need trimming to keep them in good shape and prevent any cracking.

Q. My horse seems to slip a lot whenever I ride him on the roads—are there any special shoes which would give him a better grip?

A. Make sure that a part of this problem is not due to your way of riding. Some roads can be treacherously slippery, so you should keep sufficient rein contact to enable him to remain well balanced,

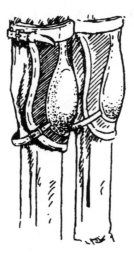

Fig. 30. Fitted knee boots.

and avoid pushing him on too fast in any gait. On roads which you know are particularly bad, stick to a steady walk if necessary, even if it takes a little longer. It would be a wise investment to buy a pair of knee boots, or use leg wraps to ride out in, in order to try and protect him against the possibility of an accident. It sounds as though your horse would also benefit tremendously from being shod with borium studs—ask your farrier about this. Make sure that he is regularly shod as well, since worn shoes provide little grip on smooth surfaces.

Q. I'm going to start competing in cross-country competitions soon— should I use studs in my horse's shoes?

A. The principle of using studs is similar to that of an athlete wearing spikes in his running shoes. Studs can be handy for all sorts of competitive work, dressage as well as show-jumping or cross-country riding. They give a better purchase on the ground; consequently the horse gains more confidence in its ability to perform whatever is required of it. They are not an absolute must, of course, as many people do compete quite successfully without them. But if you wish to achieve the best possible performance from your horse, they can give you that extra bit of advantage when the ground conditions are not ideal.

Ask your farrier to put stud holes in your horse's shoes the next time he is shod; you will be able to buy the studs themselves either from him, or from a tack shop. Use pointed studs for hard surfaces, square ones for soft surfaces, while if it is springy, small studs should be used in all four shoes for dressage, but large dome-shaped ones for jumping and cross-country. The choice can be bewildering if you are not familiar with them, so you should ask your farrier or tack shop for advice if you are not sure about which you want. When jumping, only put studs in the outside heels of the back shoes, as there is less chance of the rider being injured by the back feet than the front ones in the event of a fall. Similarly, if the studs are in the outside heels, the horse will not injure himself so badly should he accidentally tread on himself.

To put the studs in, you will need a tap, a wrench, an old shoeing nail, and the studs you have decided to use. Clean the stud holes out first using the nail, and then the tap—this has a thread

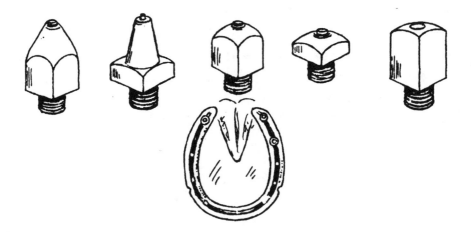

Fig. 31. Different types of studs.

on it the same size as the hole, and will clear the threads and ensure that the stud goes in more easily. Then screw the stud in, using the wrench to tighten it up, and taking care to ensure that it is straight, not at an angle. When the competition is over, remove the studs again unless they are designed to stay there permanently. Competition studs are unsuitable for roadwork and the like, and they will not only cause the horse to work lopsidedly on a hard surface, but are likely to shear off besides.

Q. When I was picking out my mare's feet the other day, I noticed that there were quite a few ragged pieces of frog hanging off. She is not lame, but will these eventually make her so, or affect her in any way? I haven't noticed them before.

A. This is quite a normal occurrence. The frog and sole of the foot are continuously producing new cells, which are normally worn away through contact with the ground. As this has not happened very effectively with your mare's feet, you should ask your farrier to trim the ragged pieces off next time he comes to shoe. This will not hurt, as it is only dead tissue; but if it is neglected, dirt could become lodged beneath the ragged pieces, and an infection, such as thrush, could arise. It might be a good idea to have a talk with your farrier anyway, as the frog may not be wearing away because it is not in contact with the ground when the horse moves. Special shoes may help. The frog should make contact with the ground, as this plays an important part in promoting the circulation of the blood in the hoof and legs.

Q. My farrier won't ever replace the old shoes when he comes to see my gelding—he always insists on putting new ones on. This is very costly; should I say something about it to him, or change to another farrier?

A. There is probably a very good reason for this; the shoes may look reasonably substantial but might in fact be quite worn, and would not last until the next visit. They could snap across the toes, or the heels wear right through, and they would not afford your horse a great deal of grip either. He will need reshoeing around every four to six weeks. If you do not ride on the roads much, you may be able to get away with using the old set once more, but if your activities involve much work on hard surfaces, they wear more quickly, and your farrier is right to recommend a new set. Make sure that your horse is not harder on his shoes than he should be by keeping him active with elevation in the stride. If you notice that he wears the toes of his back shoes out more quickly than his front ones, get your vet to examine him, as it could be a sign of the onset of navicular disease.

Q. My horse dishes quite badly; is there any corrective shoeing which can be performed to correct this trait?

A. There is little that can be done about "dishing" (the front feet swinging outward as the animal moves). If you try to correct it by shoeing, to change the natural angle of the foot to the ground, you may place strain on the joints and inner structures. If your horse is young, there is a good chance that as he grows older and stronger, the characteristic will lessen.

Q. I have noticed that my horse is not moving so well now that the ground has become so hard. His stride is noticeably shorter and more stilted and he moves far less freely and is hesitant when jumping, which is very unlike him. Could there be something wrong with his shoes?

A. You should have him examined by the vet in case there is a more deep-seated problem here, although by the sound of it, the hard ground is jarring his legs and feet and causing him some discomfort. What he is feeling when he is jumping is similar to the sensation you receive when jumping off a wall with your legs braced, instead of flexing them. As you can imagine, this would become quite painful after a while. Reduce the amount of work you are doing on hard surfaces, even if it does mean having to miss a few shows. It is more important to keep your horse sound for the future than to risk him for the sake of a few ribbons. While the ground remains so hard, it would be best if you could carry out serious schooling and jumping on the more yielding surface of an indoor school. If you inquire locally, you should find that it is possible to rent the use of one at a reasonable price from a nearby riding school or boarding stable. Particularly if he is young, you must remember that too much work on hard ground could damage his legs, and even result in permanent unsoundness. Regarding shoeing, have a word with your farrier about the possibility of shoeing him with some form of hoof cushion to absorb some of the concussion.

Q. Due to a hectic work schedule for the next two months, I am planning to turn my horse out to grass for some time off. Should I continue keeping him shod, or have his shoes taken off altogether?

A. If your horse's feet are in good condition, you could remove his shoes altogether if you wish, although they will still need attention from your farrier to keep them right. As it is only a short time, you might feel it is preferable to keep your horse shod (especially if his hooves are prone to cracking at all). If he is unused to being turned out, or kicks, then it is always best to leave the back shoes off altogether. Your farrier is probably the best person to consult about your horse's feet, as he will be most familiar with their condition, and will be able to advise you on the best course of action to take.

Q. Is there anything I should do to prepare for when the farrier arrives to shoe my new horse?

A. If possible, try to be present when the farrier is shoeing, as he may want you to hold your horse if he is awkward, rather than tying him up. This may occasionally be inconvenient; so if other people share your pasture, you will find it mutually beneficial to share this chore, since you will then be able to take turns handling the horses for the farrier. Make sure that you catch your horse in plenty of time so the farrier does not have to wait.

If you are unable to be around and nobody else is prepared to bring him in for you, then you will have to leave him stabled, or in a smaller and closer field. The farrier will not appreciate having to tramp across to the far side of a muddy fifty-acre field—in fact, he is just as likely to turn around and go home in disgust. If you are able to leave him in, then give his feet a good scrub and dry them as well as you are able to, as this will make the job easier and more pleasant. The farrier will probably also appreciate the offer of a cup of coffee, and prompt payment too!

Q. My horse tends to have very dry, brittle feet which crack easily, so that he tends to keep losing his shoes. What can be done about this?

A. Although your horse's feet should not be allowed to become overlong, if he is shod too frequently the hoof wall will become weakened due to the number of holes made by the nails. Have a talk with your farrier to see if it is possible to leave the shoes on a bit longer.

There are certain conditions which are likely to remove the varnish secreted by the periopic band at the top of the hoof wall. This coats the hoof's walls and prevents the evaporation of moisture. Its absence causes the horn to become dry and brittle. These conditions include working in salty areas (indoor schools can often contain a large quantity of salt to prevent the surface from becoming too dry and dusty), sandy areas, or if the horse is bedded on shavings or sawdust.

The feet should also be washed with cold water and a soft water brush when they become caked with mud, since the grit will also scratch if it is allowed to remain.

Protect the hooves by coating them daily (once they are clean) with one of the many brands of hoof grease available from the tack shop. A feed supplement containing biotin or methionine will improve the quality of horn growth from within, although it will take months of continuous use before you see any change.

Q. My horse seems to be particularly prone to bruising her soles, which means that she spends some time off work each time this happens. Is there anything that the farrier could do about this?

A. Horses with thin or flat rather than concave soles tend to be more liable to bruising, which can be very uncomfortable. Ask your farrier if he feels that shoeing with pads would be beneficial. Remember also that corns are another form of bruising, and are likely to lead to lameness. The cause may be small stones becoming wedged between the heel of the shoe and hoof. Perhaps the heels of the shoes are too long or too short. Frequently, the shoes are left on for too long, so do make sure that your horse is shod regularly.

Q. The other day my farrier commented on the fact that my horse brushes, and suggested that next time he comes, he puts on brushing boots. What exactly are these?

A. "Brushing" occurs when the inside of one hoof strikes against the fetlock or hoof of the opposite leg (e.g., left hind brushing the

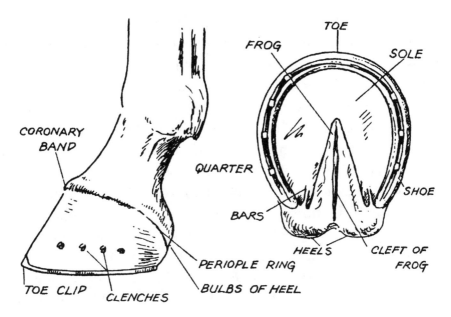

CORONARY BAND

TOE CLIP

CLENCHES

PERIOPLE RING

BULBS OF HEEL

FROG

TOE

SOLE

QUARTER

BARS

HEELS

CLEFT OF FROG

SHOE

Fig. 32. Parts of the foot and shoe.

right hind). A protective brushing boot buckled around the fetlock will prevent injury.

Q. How can I tell whether my horse is being well shod or not?

A. One of the most important things is that the shoe has been made to fit the foot, not vice versa. It should also appear to be of the right size and weight for the animal and the type of work which it is expected to do. A heavy shoe is unsuitable for a small pony, while too light a one will quickly be worn out by a heavy horse. On close inspection, you should see that the shoe also meets the hoof wall exactly, otherwise dirt and grit can work their way upward, creating an infection; it will also create an uneven pressure on the weight-bearing surfaces of the foot, which could result in structural damage. The traditional number of nails used is seven—four on the outside and three on the inside, but fewer may be used if the foot is small, or the walls thin, or the animal is inclined to brush. The nails themselves come in various sizes and are used according to the size of the animal being shod. Too large a nail can lead to cracking, while too small a nail gives insufficient grip, and movement will occur between shoe and hoof, eventually resulting in the shank of the nail breaking and the shoe becoming loose. Look at the nail heads; after shoeing they should lie flush with the shoe if the correct size of nail has been used.

One of the easiest points to check for yourself is the accuracy of the nailing. If the horse has good feet, the clenches—the points where the ends of the nails appear through the hoof walls and are turned down to form a hook to hold the shoe in place—should be in a straight line, rather than at uneven heights with some lower or higher than others. The height of the clenches should be approximately one-third of the way up the wall of the hoof. It is more difficult for the layperson to determine whether the hoof itself is prepared correctly; but the "bars" of the hoof (the parts of the hoof wall that turn in toward the frog) should never be cut away, as they have a vital role to play as part of the surface supporting the horse's weight, in absorbing concussion, and helping to return blood from the hoof and up the leg. Look at the angle of the hoof; you should be able to note that its slope is the same as that of the pastern. If this line is broken, stresses are then placed unequally, not just within the hoof, but the leg as well.

There is not a lot that a farrier can do for a hoof that is badly shaped due to hereditary conformation. Here he should shoe to the shape of the hoof rather than trying to make it conform to the ideal; the horse is more likely to remain sound with this method.

Watch how your horse is handled; a farrier who is firm but quiet is far more likely to do a good job than one who is abrupt, upsets the horse, and then has trouble getting the shoe on because the animal won't stand still.

Your horse should be shod regularly; a farrier cannot be held to blame for hooves in poor condition if you have neglected to call him in the first place! Most farriers are only too pleased to explain a little about their trade and what they are doing if you express an interest in it, so do not be afraid to ask questions.

Q. What is the best way of removing a shoe if it becomes loose?

A. If the shoe is very loose, or has twisted so that it is in danger of injuring your horse, you can remove it yourself. Ask your farrier to demonstrate this, along with how to hold up both front and back feet so that you will be well prepared in the event of an emergency. Ask him if he will sell you an old rasp and some pincers—or you could even make do with what you have in the toolbox. The easiest way to remove the shoe is to rasp the clenches away first so that you do not pull any of the hoof away as you remove the shoe. Once all of the clenches have been rasped down, place the pincers at the outside heel of the shoe. Get the jaws as far beneath it as you can, and holding them firmly, lever downward and slightly in toward the toe. As the shoe begins to come away, repeat the procedure on the inside heel, then return to the outside and carry on working the shoe off from each side in turn, finishing at the toe.

10

Veterinary Problems

Q. I have a light chestnut pony whose nose gets sunburned in the summer—it cracks and gets very red and sore. Is there anything I can put on it to stop this from happening, as it looks very painful?

A. Light-colored horses and ponies, and those with light-colored or pink muzzles, can be quite prone to sunburn. Try using a sunblock or lip balm when he is turned out, and put calamine lotion on to help soothe the skin. You might also consider stabling him during the daytime when the sun is at its hottest; the shelter from flies will probably be appreciated just as much as the relief from the heat.

Q. Recently I have noticed that my horse is taking longer than usual to eat his feed, and I sometimes find chewed-up bits of hay lying beneath his haynet, as though he has spit them out. Is he being fussy, or could he be feeling unwell?

A. Since your horse is still eating up his feed, it sounds more likely that he is suffering from sharp teeth, which are causing him some discomfort when he is chewing. As a result, he is dropping pieces of half-chewed food from his mouth, which will mean that he gets neither his full ration, nor a great deal of benefit from that which he does swallow. It could also be due to other types of mouth ailments; lampas (an inflammation of the soft palate), mouth ulcers, or an abscess. Ask your vet to do a proper check for you. Remember to have your horse's teeth checked every six months anyway, and rasped, or floated, as needed, since sharp edges could cause lacerations of the tongue and mouth, creating difficulties not only in eating, but when riding too.

Q. A friend had a look at my horse's teeth the other day, and reckoned that he is older than I thought he was. How exactly can you tell the age by looking at the teeth?

A. It is possible to estimate a horse's age with a reasonable amount of accuracy until it reaches 8 years old, when it is said to be "aged." After this, it is a matter of guesswork. Even with a younger animal, you should still bear in mind that all individuals may vary slightly from the given pattern of tooth growth and development. Environment, breeding, feeding, general health, and conformation will all play a part in altering the way in which the teeth become worn. The teeth you look at to determine a horse's age are the incisors, or the front teeth, which are used for biting off grass. There are six of these in each jaw, given the names centrals, laterals, and corners, according to their positions. The surface where the top and bottom sets of teeth meet is referred to as the table; in a younger horse, the enamel around the edges of each tooth's table is seen to be higher than the black centers, giving the effect of a shallow cavity. As the animal grows older, this cavity becomes shallower, until the surfaces of the teeth are flat. The older the horse becomes, the longer the teeth also appear to be, and the more acute the angle at which they meet; the black

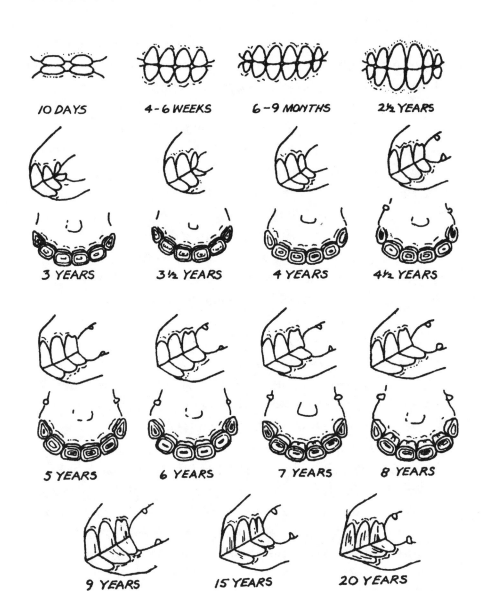

Fig. 33. Stages of ageing in teeth.

marks in the centers of the tables also become smaller and rounder. As an approximate guide, you should be able to see the teeth in the following stages of wear and tear at these ages:

10 days	two central milk teeth are cut
4–10 weeks	the lateral incisors are cut
6–9 months	the corner incisors are cut
2½ years	the central milk teeth are replaced by permanent teeth (these are longer and larger with a less rounded gum line)
3 years	the central incisors begin to wear (the upper and lower teeth meet)
3½ years	the lateral incisors are replaced by permanent teeth
4 years	the lateral incisors begin to wear
4½ years	the corner incisors are cut
4½ years	the canine teeth or "tushes" erupt in males
5 years	the corner incisors begin to wear, and the horse is said to have a "full mouth"
6 years	the cavity in the central incisors disappears
7 years	the cavity in the lateral incisors disappears
7 years	a hook may form on the edge of the corners; it develops and recedes gradually, starting to disappear by the end of the year
8 years	the cavity in the corner incisors disappears

After this point, ageing becomes difficult to estimate with any accuracy; at about nine years old a mark appears close to the gum on the upper corner incisors, and gradually extends downward. This is called "Galvayne's groove." At about fifteen years it extends halfway down the length of the tooth, and down the entire length at about twenty years old. After this it gradually disappears, and the only indication of age in an old horse is the length and angle of the teeth, and the wearing of the tables.

Q. My horse has a front tooth missing; is this going to cause problems?

A. Where a tooth has been lost, there will be nothing to wear down the surface of the opposite one, and so you should make sure that it is kept rasped level with the others on the same jaw. Your vet should keep an eye on it.

Q. My mare is just recovering from an illness, and the vet has told me that I can now start turning her out again. How should I go about getting her used to this? I don't want her to injure herself tearing around the first time she goes out.

A. It is best to make sure that when you first turn her out she is hungry, so that she is likely to settle down more quickly to grazing. If possible, and if you think it will be beneficial to her, try and provide a quiet companion who will help her to settle. It is advisable to turn her out in a small paddock to start with, as this will discourage her from galloping around quite so madly—particularly if you are able to find somewhere to put her where she will be well away from other horses (other than her companion) whose presence could cause her to get over-excited. When you let her go, turn her head to the gate, so that she is unable to kick out at you the moment you release her. Leave the gate slightly ajar so that you are able to slip behind it quickly. Releasing her is best accomplished if you leave the halter on, and loop a long lead rope through it, rather than clipping it on. All you have to do then is simply slip the rope free.

If you are very worried about the possibility of her injuring herself, have a talk with your vet, who may advise giving her a mild sedative just beforehand. Do not leave her out for too long at first, but gradually build up the length of time she is out, as the change in her diet once she is grazing again could upset her stomach if the changeover is too sudden.

Q. My horse is plagued by flies in the summer months—is there a really effective repellent I can use for him?

A. Flies seem to be particularly attracted to dirty and sweating horses, and you may find that regular bathing will help to lessen his appeal to them, particularly if you shampoo him with a product which has a mild antiseptic included in it. If you are unable to bathe him properly after riding, a quick wash-down with water and sponge will certainly help. When flies are at their worst, your horse is unlikely to settle down to grazing, so you could also try stabling during the daytime; put up some flypapers to provide the best deterrent from them. When he does go out, or if you are

Fig. 34. Horses standing in the shade, nose to tail.

Fig. 35. A fitted fly scrim.

unable to stable him, it is ideal if he has some shelter and the companionship of another pony or horse, as they will be able to stand nose to tail and provide a mutual fly-swatting service.

Try to avoid pulling tails or forelocks, and allow the tail to grow to a reasonable length. If the forelock is on the thin side, you could also buy a fly scrim or mask, which attaches to the halter, or under the jaw with Velcro. Many effective commercial insect repellents are available from tack shops, but you will also find that home remedies like citronella and white vinegar work well. Feeding two chopped cloves of garlic also seems to help lessen the problem; as the horse sweats, the odor acts as a natural repellent.

Q. Just recently my Thoroughbred-cross mare's coat has started to grow through lighter in the area where her saddle patch is. Her saddle fits her well—tack shop personnel have checked its fit. I was planning to show her this summer, but she looks rather odd. Is there any reason for this, or anything I can do to prevent it from getting worse?

A. This discoloration seems to happen quite frequently in horses with TB blood. Other than making sure the saddle fits correctly, there is not a great deal you can do about it, except to massage the saddle area after removing the saddle to ensure the return of normal blood circulation. As far as showing is concerned, it is possible to obtain different shades of hair dye which you could use to disguise the saddle patch. Try a small test area first, to check match of color and that there are no skin reactions.

Q. My horse had a sore back last year, and the area which was rubbed has now healed up nicely. However, the hairs are now growing through white—will these turn back to brown eventually?

A. You should, of course, try to prevent the rubbing from happening again, and check and correct the saddle, the pad, or whatever the object was that caused the injury. It was obviously serious enough to damage the pigmentation cells, and now that the hairs have grown through white, they are there to stay.

Q. My pony has got broken wind. What can I do to keep him as comfortable as possible?

A. Any horse or pony with a cough or respiratory problem needs a good system of stable management. His environment needs to be kept as dust-free as possible, so that the condition is not aggravated. The top doors of stables should never be closed, but left open so that the area is well ventilated, and he should be turned out on grass as much as possible, where he will be in the fresh air. When mucking out, the animal should be turned out, or transferred to another stable, and any dust left to settle before putting him back.

Straw is not the ideal bedding, as it not only can be dusty, but is frequently eaten, distending the stomach which presses on the lungs. A substitute should be found, such as shredded paper or very clean wood shavings. These can be dampened down slightly by sprinkling the bed with diluted disinfectant. This will keep dust to a minimum, and also prevent any harmful nibbling due to its unpleasant taste. Hay should be soaked for twenty-four hours, or alternatively, a brand of dust- and spore-free hay should be fed. All feeds should be dampened, and a cough mixture given to help soothe the throat if a cough is present.

Grooming is best done outdoors, with the animal's head facing into the wind. Generally speaking, the better fit you can keep the pony, the better able to cope it will be; your vet will be able to advise you as to a limited exercise routine. Any horse or pony that is coughing (other than simply clearing its nose on the start of exercise) should not, however, be worked. The vet should be consulted at once.

Q. My horse's feet are very smelly, and there is a small amount of greasy, black-colored discharge coming from the frog area. He is not lame—is this a normal condition?

A. The condition described is thrush, and if neglected could eventually lead to lameness. It arises through standing in wet, dirty, or muddy conditions, and from the feet not being picked out regularly enough. Keep stable bedding as clean as possible, muck out frequently if your horse spends much time standing indoors, and with plenty of fresh clean bedding put down each day. Pick the feet out at least twice a day, and treat with a drying agent such as Coppertox, formalin bleach, or Betadine in the early stages, or magnesium sulfate in more advanced cases.

Q. A friend's horse had colic recently, and nearly died from it. What should I do if my horse gets an attack? And what are the first symptoms?

A. The symptoms vary considerably, depending on the type and cause of colic; the horse will generally appear distressed and uncomfortable. If stabled, the bedding may show signs of rolling, or the horse's restlessness. The top lip often is curled back; it may kick at its stomach, or turn to look at it. It may just stand looking dejected, or in violent cases it will lie down and roll. The horse may be sweating, off its feed, have a tight, staring coat, and be straining to pass urine or droppings, but without success. Small, mucous-covered droppings may be visible in the bed, or alternatively, the animal may be suffering from diarrhea.

If it is a blockage-type of colic, there will be little or no bowel movement if you place your ear to the flanks; it is not a bad idea to be familiar with the normal rumbling that can be heard. If it is an enteritis-type colic, there will on the other hand be an excessive amount of noise, and weight will quickly be lost; the horse quickly becoming visibly thinner. The horse may also rinse its mouth frequently with water, but without actually taking a drink.

On recognizing any of these symptoms, and suspecting colic, you should call your vet immediately, describing the behavior and how long it has been going on. While you are waiting for him to arrive, try to make the horse as comfortable as possible, although should the symptoms become violent, you should take care of your own safety too. Put him in a large airy stall with plenty of bedding that has been well banked up around the walls. If he is cold, put on stable bandages, and a blanket with an anti-sweat sheet beneath in case he begins to sweat. Leave the front straps undone, so that he is more comfortable; should the blankets slip, he will not become entangled in them, they will simply drop free. Leave a halter on in case you need to catch hold of him quickly. Allow him to lie down if he is happier like that, but do not allow him to roll; if he does try this, either get him back on his feet again, or sit on his neck just behind his head to keep him still, so that he does not injure himself internally in his struggles.

Q. I am getting a medicine cabinet together for my horse; what should I stock it with?

A. If you are worried about your horse's health at any time, you should call the vet immediately, rather than meddling and perhaps making the situation worse. However, it doesn't hurt to have a few first aid things around, so that in the event of an emergency, you are at least able to cope until qualified assistance arrives. If your horse looks a little off, it will also enable you to check up on him, and deal with minor problems. Keep all the things together; old drugs should be discarded rather than saved once they have served their purpose, and the entire box should be kept well out of the reach of animals or young children. The following items should be included (check with your vet for any other items to include):

- Veterinary thermometer
- Epsom salts
- Table salt
- Scissors
- Bandages (stable and gauze)
- Vaseline or other poultices
- Antiseptic cream
- Antibiotic powder and ointment
- Rubbing alcohol
- Hydrogen peroxide
- Witch-hazel
- Wound dressing
- Zinc oxide
- Boric acid
- Tincture of iodine (or other disinfectant)
- Hoof dressing
- Liniment

- Instant cold pack
- Soaking tub, access to cold water hose
- Hot pack
- Mineral oil (for treating colic)
- Measuring cup and spoon
- Fly repellent
- Twitch (for restraint)
- Towels
- Flashlight

Q. How should I deal with simple cuts, and which ones should I call the vet to treat?

A. The first thing you must do if your horse cuts himself is to assess the seriousness of the injury, and whether it is likely to need more experienced help and treatment. These instances are:

- If a cut looks as though it will need stitching
- If a vein or artery has been nicked or severed
- If a joint has been damaged (other than minor cuts)
- If a bone is broken, or suspected to be
- If an anti-tetanus booster is required
- Or any occasion when you feel that you are unable to treat an injury competently yourself.

If a vein or artery has been damaged, you should try to stop the bleeding until the vet comes. In the case of arterial bleeding (identified by its bright red color, which spurts since it is still under the pumping influence of the heart), you should press a clean pad firmly over the area and apply digital pressure. Veinous bleeding (maroon in color and a steady flow) is best treated by running a hose at low pressure over the injury to constrict the blood vessels, thereby lessening the amount of blood lost. If a bone is broken, then no pressure should be applied other than a low-pressure hose if necessary to stop bleeding, and the animal should not be moved. The types of cuts which you are most likely to encounter are:

Punctures—These are caused by a pointed object such as a thorn or nail, and can be quite dangerous since the wound is often deeper than at first suspected, and sometimes escapes notice altogether. If the object is still embedded, it should be carefully removed, noting the depth and angle to which it has penetrated, and the wound should then be poulticed to remove any possible source of infection.

Abrasions—These are grazes, often occurring as a result of jumping solid fences, or falling on the road. The area should be cleaned as thoroughly as possible, and then poulticed, as it is likely that dirt will have become worked in.

Incisions—These clean cuts may be caused by broken glass. Unless they are very deep, bleeding is usually minimal, and provided they are properly cleaned and treated regularly with an antiseptic cream, are unlikely to cause very much trouble.

Contusions—This is a bruise where the skin is not broken, but appears as a direct result of a blow—possibly a kick from another horse or pony. Tissues and blood vessels have become broken, giving rise to a warm, tender swelling. Alternating hot and cold poultices or compresses is usually the best way to repair the damage and reduce the swelling.

Lacerations—Tear wounds can be quite serious, many arising because of poor maintenance of barbed-wire fencing. They may also occur when a bone shatters, and splinters are forced outward from within, breaking through the skin. There is often quite a bit of bleeding, since a large number of blood vessels have been damaged. The injury should be treated carefully, hosing with a low-pressure hose to clean it. If stitching is needed, the vet should be called promptly if the wound is to close up satisfactorily. If the cut is fairly minor, then treating with antiseptic cream after cleaning is usually quite adequate.

Over-reach—This happens when the toe of a back foot catches the heel of a front foot, inflicting a cut. It may be overlooked at first, as a flap of skin may conceal the injury. The flap of dead skin should be cut off first of all, so that the area can be easily treated, and dirt does not become trapped beneath. After hosing it free of dirt, it should then be poulticed, until clean. Afterwards a dry dressing can be used until the injury has healed over sufficiently to prevent dirt getting in.

The most effective way of cleaning a cut is to hose it, since this is less likely to work dirt in. If the injury is in an area where hosing may be difficult or impossible to manage, then a piece of cotton wool may be soaked in salty water and squeezed out over it. Disinfectants should not be used as they are likely to retard healing; salty water is a far better antiseptic wash. If the legs need to be hosed frequently in order to keep a cut clean, the heels should be coated in petroleum jelly to keep them from chapping or cracking.

The best way to clean a hoof injury, such as a punctured sole, is to soak the foot in a bucket or tub. The hoof should be picked out and scrubbed to remove the worst of the dirt. The heels should be smeared with petroleum jelly, and then the hoof can be held above a shallow bucket to which clean hot water and a double handful of Epsom salts have been added. A little of the water should be ladled over the hoof, accustoming the horse to the temperature, before gently lowering the hoof into the bucket. It may be useful to have an assistant pick up the opposite leg in order to discourage fidgeting around during this process. From time to time as the water cools, the bucket should be topped up again with more hot water, but the level should never be allowed to rise above the coronary band, or else instead of being drawn out of the hoof, dirt and infection will be drawn upward. Soaking should continue for about twenty minutes, after which the hoof can be dried and poulticed. It should be soaked again each time before poulticing.

Q. I have just bought a pony which had an attack of laminitis two years ago. I am worried that he may get it again; what should I do to try and prevent it?

A. Laminitis is an acutely painful condition for any pony, and precautions should be taken to prevent its occurrence in animals most likely to be susceptible, and the recurrence in those that have been affected before. The condition itself is an inflammation of the sensitive laminae of the hoof—these are fine tissue-like structures which support the pedal bone and contain large amounts of blood. With the onset of laminitis, these laminae begin to break down, and if the situation is allowed to become very bad, the pedal bone may begin to drop downward, until it penetrates the sole of the hoof. By the time this stage has been reached, the animal is usually in considerable pain, and the kindest option is to have it put out of its misery. There are a number of causes: too much work on hard surfaces, following an attack of colic or after foaling, being given a cold drink when hot. It has most frequently come to be associated with both horses and ponies that are overweight, under-exercised, and on too rich a diet. The symptoms are a reluctance to move around, lying down for unusually long periods of time, standing with the weight on the heels, and a raised temperature, which may be accompanied by sweating and warm or hot feet. A swollen sheath or udder can sometimes give an early warning, since it is often symptomatic of an overfed animal that is not exercised sufficiently. The moment you notice any of these signs, particularly since your pony has suffered before, you should notify the vet.

Best of all, you should attempt to prevent the onset. Restrict the grazing, particularly during the spring and autumn flushes of grass. This may be done by either fencing off an area of the field, moving to a barer paddock, or stabling for part of the day. Do not allow the pony to become overweight, but try to keep him a little on the lean side. Exercise regularly, since this will also help to stop him from becoming overweight, and be sure to stick to the minimum necessary amount of pelleted feed for the work he is doing. He should be regularly shod every four to six weeks too, so that his heels do not become overlong, as this could lead to bad circulation back up the leg from the foot.

Fig. 36. A laminitic pony—the typical stance, with its weight on its heels.

Q. My pony has started to rub his mane and tail a lot; is this just due to the fact that the weather is getting warmer and he is changing his coat?

A. This could be due either to lice or to summer eczema. Lice will be noticed during the spring months, and look very much like small hayseeds. These can be eliminated by sprinkling a louse powder along the roots of the mane on both sides, along the spine, and on the tail. This should be repeated two weeks later. Check up on the last date of worming too, as worm infestation can cause irritation around the anus.

The other possibility is that it could signify the onset of summer eczema. This is a form of non-contagious dermatitis which causes intense irritation; affected animals will often rub the areas along the crest, withers, and top of the dock until they are raw and bleeding. It is thought that the cause is an allergic reaction to cer-

Fig. 37. A pony affected by summer eczema, with its rubbed mane and tail.

tain biting midges, and it seems to be most common in cold-blooded types and those kept outdoors. The condition will occur during the spring and summer months, often continuing well into the autumn if the weather is mild. No cure has yet been discovered, and treatment consists mainly of prevention as far as possible, and the use of drugs and lotions aimed at relieving the discomfort. As soon as the weather gets warmer, you should stable your pony during the daytime, only turning him out once it is dark—twilight and early morning especially are bad times for midges and to be avoided, but bright sunlight also seems to aggravate the situation. Fly repellents should be used, and a fly strip can be hung up in the stable. Bathing the affected areas frequently with cold water seems to ease matters, and calamine lotion, benzyl benzoate, or one of the sweet-itch lotion brand-name products can be used to provide relief and stimulation of hair regrowth. You should also consult your vet, as he may be able to administer antihistamine or cortisone injections.

Q. When should I call the vet?

A. At any time when your horse or pony appears to be unwell, and also for routine checkups. His teeth should be checked every six months, and he should be covered by all annual vaccinations. If he is lame, has a cough, or shows any signs of worrisome abnormal behavior, you should also call the vet. When looking at a horse in good health, its general attitude should be one of alertness, and yet relaxation, and of general well-being, covered with plenty of flesh without actually being overweight. It should stand and move comfortably, with no signs of lameness. Taking a closer look, the eyes should be bright, with no signs of discharge. The mucous membranes of both eyes, nostrils, and gums, should be salmon pink in color. A yellowish tinge indicates jaundice; red, a fever; a bluish-red tinge, heart trouble; and pale membranes, anemia.

There should be no discharge from the nostrils, other than perhaps a small amount of clear nasal discharge; if it increases in quantity, becomes thick, or discolored, it indicates the presence of infection.

The appetite should be good, but normal—not eating voraciously, but neither picking at, or leaving, food. There should be no trouble in mastication. The limbs should all be free from unusual lumps and bumps. The coat should lie flat, with a healthy sheen on it; a tight coat is an indication of ill health, and often accompanies worm infestation and malnutrition. The urine should be nearly colorless and free of offensive odor, while the droppings should be firm and rounded, just breaking slightly as they hit the ground. Small, hard droppings coated with mucous may indicate constipation and worms, while diarrhea is often due to a digestive upset or gut irritation. The horse should not sweat (unless he has just been exercised hard). A hot sweat without such justification indicates pain, an elevated temperature, or a fever, while a cold sweat may break out if there is pain or mental disturbance.

The temperature in a healthy horse or pony should be approximately 100 to 101.5 degrees Fahrenheit, although this may vary slightly from one individual to another, and according to the time of year, so it is important to know what is right for your own particular animal. The temperature may be taken by shaking down a veterinary thermometer, lubricating the bulb with a little liquid paraffin or petroleum jelly, and then inserting it into the rectum for a minute and a half. It should be angled slightly so that it rests against the bowel wall, and not in the middle of a ball of feces. Ask an assistant to hold the horse throughout, as some are not cooperative about the procedure. After use, disinfect the thermometer and put it away again, ready for future use. A rise in temperature of two or three degrees above normal means that pain is present; if higher, that there is an infection. Respiration should be around

8 to 12 inhalations/exhalations per minute in a normal horse standing at rest. Stand slightly to the back and one side of the quarters in order to see the movement of the flanks quite clearly. Count each time that they either move in or out. The pulse should be in the region of 35 to 40 per minute. It can be felt anywhere that an artery crosses a bone, but the easiest place is probably just beneath the jawbone, in front of the cheek.

11

Shows

Q. How can I find out where local shows are being held?

A. Each year the weekly magazine *The Chronicle of the Horse* publishes a show directory, and USA Equestrian (formerly the American Horse Shows Association) lists its recognized horse shows in an annual calendar. You can also check with breed and activity organizations for their listings. Most horse magazines publish advertisements for shows, while smaller, more local events are often publicized in the local press. It is always worth inquiring at local tack shops, riding schools, and regional riding groups for local (and largely unrecognized) shows.

Q. I'd like to do some cross-country competitions with my youngster, but I don't really think he is quite ready for the pressure of a proper competition. How can I give him some experience without actually having to enter a class?

A. Some cross-country competitions will allow you to enter your horse *hors de concours,* which means the horse participates but won't be scored. This would give you both the opportunity of gaining experience under show conditions, but without the pressure.

Fig. 38. A horse jumping a cross-country fence (being watched by another rider).

Q. I am taking my young son and his pony to participate in a leading rein class at a local show shortly. Should the lead rein be clipped to the bit or the nose band?

A. The lead rein should be clipped to the nose band, and the pony seen to be moving freely forward and in response to his rider, rather than having to be restrained or dragged along by the person leading.

Q. My horse has a great deal of ability in show-jumping, and I would now like to enter him in some recognized shows—how do I go about doing this?

A. You will need to be a member of USA Equestrian (formerly the American Horse Shows Association), and your horse will also need to be registered with them. If you are not a member, you

Fig. 39.
(a) The correct way to attach a lead rein in lead rein classes.
(b) A pony in a lead rein class.

must pay a non-member fee for each class you enter. Further information can be obtained, (see chapter 16).

Q. I would like to take up show-jumping more seriously, but am finding it very expensive by the time I have paid for traveling and entry fees. How should I go about finding a sponsor so that I can carry on?

A. Nowadays, when it is becoming increasingly expensive to keep a horse, let alone to compete with it on a regular basis, everybody is on the lookout for a sponsor. When approaching a possible sponsor, you should first remember to aim at sponsorship suitable to the level of competition you intend to do. If you are going to be riding at local riding club shows, your best bet is to approach small local firms rather than large nationwide ones. There is no point in tackling a large company unless you have a good track record riding in affiliated competition, as a big company will be more interested in nationwide publicity. Often, for a competitor who does not command the sort of following and publicity which top international riders can muster, it is more successful to approach a small local company and compete in shows in the area.

To have any success in finding a sponsor, you will have to do some footwork first. Rather than just writing and hoping for a favorable reply to your suggestions, it is often best to make an appointment and call in for a personal visit. Do not exclude any firm as being too small—you could check out the possibility of assistance from grocery stores or small firms that trade in your area. At the interview you will need to try and make the right sort of impression, and sound very confident of your abilities.

You will need to show some kind of documentation at this meeting—it is not enough to simply tell your sponsor how good your horse is going to be. It must already have demonstrated ability and success. It will help if you can produce a record of your achievements, preferably with the horse which you would like sponsored, backed up if possible with a few good photographs of the two of you in action at a show. Know what kind of deal you are after. Prepare a list of future shows, their dates, venues, and how many classes you will enter at each. Decide on what expenses you are likely to incur, and what percentage you would ideally like your sponsor to cover. It might be best to settle for travel expenses initially. Don't be greedy, as a small firm won't be able to afford the expense—you have to compete favorably with the sort of publicity to be gained from placing an ad in the local newspaper. It is better to have a little help than none at all, and it will prove that you are sufficiently sure of your capabilities if you are willing to put up some of your own cash.

Of course, sponsorship is a two-way arrangement; you will hope to benefit from it, but so does your sponsor. Point out that the cost of your traveling, for example, works out at less than the price of an ad in the local paper; and remind them of the wide range of people you will be seen by. It is not solely horse people who go to shows; they frequently become family outings as well. You will have to be prepared to wear the company or store's logo or name on your blankets, and will have to decide who will keep the trophies and ribbons (it is usually only fair that the sponsor keeps them). You will also need to come to some agreement about any prize money (whether you will retain it or divide it). It is best to have something in writing about these points to avoid dispute in the future.

If you manage to gain sponsorship, you will also have to make the effort to be polite, cheerful, and helpful to everyone you speak to, so that you promote your sponsor's image, rather than destroy it. You will in effect be on show as a sort of spokesman on their behalf. At all times both you and your horse will have to display immaculate appearance and turnout, and prove to be a good sportsman.

Q. I would like to take my four-year-old to some shows. She has quite an excitable nature, though—how can I make her first shows as quiet an introduction as possible?

A. Preparation plays a large part in making first shows trouble-free. If you are planning on transporting her in a truck or trailer, make sure that she is familiar with everything, from being bandaged up to actually traveling. The more she feels at home, the better—a battle in the middle of a showground will unsettle her. Work her occasionally with other horses, so that she is less distracted by them. On the day of the show, try to leave early; if you are riding there, it will help to take the edge off and settle her down. If traveling in a truck or trailer, give her some exercise before setting off. Select quiet classes to start with, such as a halter or conformation class, where she will only be required to walk around. Such classes are also normally the first ones on the schedule, which will suit your purposes, as the showground is unlikely to be too busy.

Give her the chance to relax and become used to the different atmosphere, whatever the type of class you are going to enter, so that she has the chance to have a good look around, and then settle down and concentrate on her work. When in a showing class, try not to get jammed in between horses, which can be an upsetting experience for a youngster. Above all, remember that you are out to start her competitive career off on the right foot, not to upset her completely. If you arrive and find that she is very uptight, just ride her quietly around for a little while, and if things don't improve, take her home again without actually going in the ring. Another day she will be better behaved for having been introduced to shows quietly and carefully. Consider other people's horses besides yours; if your mare causes a riot, nobody will be very happy at the end of the day.

Q. I want to enter some gymkhana classes with my new pony, but I am not sure what you have to do for each one. What is involved? Is there any special schooling needed? My mother said she would like to try some too (she exercises my pony to keep him fit while I am at school). Is she too old?

A. It would be a good idea to go to a gymkhana just to watch, as you can pick up a lot of tips by watching more experienced riders, as well as learning about the races. It is something that your mother can have a try at too, since there are usually different heats for different age groups, including one for adults. Since the races can be pretty tiring, though, it would be best if you rode in different races rather than the same ones. Since your mother is also able to exercise your pony, she should also be able to keep him pretty fit—you will be surprised just how much energy he will need. Do not forget your own fitness—try skipping, running, bicycling, or swimming so that you do not tire too quickly. You can also practice plenty of dismounted exercises, such as participating in a sack race (the trick is to stick a toe in each corner of the sack and run, rather than hop!). Teach your pony to lead freely in hand, and try to ensure that he is as supple and obedient as possible. Practice standing starts, vaulting on and off, and set out rows of cones or oil drums to practice bending and turning around. There are quite a few different gymkhana games, and the rules seem to vary slightly from one show to another. Your local U.S. Pony Club will have helpful information for you. Most people are quite happy to help if you are at all confused—and do watch the heat before you!

Q. I would like to be better at gymkhana classes. The trouble is that I can't vault on, so I lose a lot of time fiddling around with my stirrups. How can I get better at this—or should I just train my pony to kneel down for me instead?

A. This is definitely something which needs to be practiced at home, rather than hoping that somehow you will manage once in the ring. Instead of trying to heave yourself on as though trying to climb a brick wall, you will find it easier if you take a large handful of mane in your left hand, stand as you would when mounting normally, then really swing your right leg over your pony's back, jumping off your left foot at the same time. If you have a somewhat large pony, it is easiest to get the knack by borrowing a friend's smaller pony to start with. Then gradually work up to a

Fig. 40. Vaulting onto a pony.

bigger pony, and start practicing vaulting on, not just in halt, but trot and canter too.

Q. If my pony canters on the wrong lead, should I stop and start again, or just carry on?

A. If you get the wrong canter lead, trot and ask again for the correct lead. To do nothing shows the judge that you may not be aware that your pony is on the wrong lead.

Q. What sort of clothes do I need to wear for horse shows?

A. Traditional hunter-seat show clothes consist of a riding jacket; "ratcatcher" shirt and choker for females, or shirt and conservative tie for males; jodhpurs and jodphur boots for youngsters, or breeches and tall boots for adults. An approved hunt cap with a chin strap is essential. Gloves are optional. Pay attention to your clothes' condition; make sure there are no creases in clothes, that

Fig. 41. Riding and hunting dress.

they are clean, and correctly worn. Unless it is very short, a girl's or woman's hair should be tied back or netted.

It is worth reading the USA Equestrian rule book or the rule book of your breed or discipline for precise information on tack and apparel. You should also attend a few horse shows to watch and pick up further tips and hints on correct turnout.

Traveling

Q. I need to hire a truck or trailer to take my pony to a show, as it is too far to ride. Where can I hire one from?

A. It is worth asking around locally, as someone near you may be going to the same show and have room in their trailer or truck for an extra passenger if you chip in some money to help pay for part of the fuel expense. Otherwise, ask at local riding schools, boarding stables, or tack shops as to a reputable horse transporter in your area—or else look in the Yellow Pages.

Q. Which side of my double trailer should I transport my horse on—right or left? Or should I take out the central partition altogether?

A. You should transport your horse on the left side of the trailer, so the horse is standing closer to the road's crown; this will ensure a steadier and more comfortable ride. The same applies when transporting two animals of different weights; place the heavier one on the left side. When transporting a single horse in a trailer (or vehicle) which is designed to carry two or more animals of that size, then you should put the partition up to prevent the horse from being thrown around, and to encourage it to stand still.

Fig. 42. A horse dressed for traveling.

Q. *I am transporting my horse to a show soon—he is supposed to be good to load and so on, so does he still need to wear protective clothing? And if so, what sort?*

A. If you have never transported your horse before, it would be wise to try a practice run before the day of the show, just to check that he really is going to behave. If he is likely to prove awkward, then at least you will know that you must leave some extra time on that morning if you are to arrive on time for your classes. You should also practice dressing him up in his traveling gear in case he has never worn any before. This can be quite a frightening experience for youngsters, especially if they have never had much handling. What you choose by way of protective clothing to guard him from knocks and bumps during the journey depends upon the weather, your expertise, and personal preferences. If it is cold and the horse is clipped, then he should wear a warm stable blanket, with an anti-sweat sheet beneath in case he starts to sweat in excitement. During the summer, a light cotton or linen summer sheet will help to keep drafts off his back without overheating him;

but take the precaution of putting an anti-sweat sheet beneath the sheet anyway.

On his legs you should put traveling bandages, with squares of absorbent gauze or cotton tissue beneath so that he is well padded against accidental bumps. It is important to bandage fairly low, as the lower regions of the legs are most likely to get hurt. Bandages will also keep his legs clean on the way to a show—(if he has white socks, chalk them before bandaging). If you are not very proficient at bandaging and find them too difficult, or your horse tends to fidget, you could put traveling boots on as an alternative. These are usually very well lined, and take only a few minutes to put on or take off, and there is no danger of accidentally injuring the horse by bandaging incorrectly. The knees and hocks can be protected by leg wraps, and if you are concerned that he may tread on himself, then put over-reach boots on all around. These are easiest to put on and remove if they are the split variety, fastened by Velcro straps. A poll guard can be put on in case he lifts his head abruptly and bangs it; if you do not wish to buy one, it is easy enough to buy a thick strip of foam rubber quite cheaply, and fasten it to the headpiece of the halter. Finally, a tail bandage should be put on to prevent the hairs of the tail from becoming broken.

Q. My horse's problem is not in being loaded, or when actually traveling—he is very well behaved and never any trouble with this. But when he is unloaded, he shoots out of the trailer in reverse, coming out very fast. How can I get him to take things more steadily, before he hurts himself?

A. First, make sure that he has plenty of protective leg wraps or bandages in case the worst happens. Practice unloading him at home, not just when you go to shows, when the atmosphere is bound to make him more tense. Check that the butt bar is strong so that you have plenty of time to lower the ramp—you do not want him to come charging out before you are ready. The ramp itself should have struts nailed across its breadth to give more grip; you could also put some rubber matting down to help prevent slipping. Put a bridle on him, which will give you a bit more control, and do not forget the power of the human voice to soothe and calm any fears that he might have. Position an assistant at the bottom of the ramp, with another ready to undo the butt bar on your command. The first assistant should be ready with a yard broom, and as the butt bar is undone, can gently rest the bristles against the quarters—this provides some incentive not to rush out. If possible, you could have some tail gates fitted, as these will keep him straight and stop him from slipping over the edge of the ramp.

Fig. 43. A broom is held ready to push against the quarters of a horse that rushes out when being unloaded. Tail gate shown on right-hand side of ramp.

Q. My horse is good while traveling, except when the trailer is standing still, at traffic lights, intersections, and so on, when she always starts kicking. If she doesn't hurt herself first, I am worried that she will damage the trailer.

A. The only answer in this case is to hobble her once she is loaded up. Make sure that they are well lined with sheepskin or cotton so that they do not chafe, and remember to take them off again before trying to unload!

Q. My pony is really stubborn about being loaded. What are the best ways of getting him to behave? Sometimes it takes hours to get him into the trailer, which means that we miss classes at shows.

A. A horse or pony which is difficult to load can be very irritating, and it is worth spending some time at home teaching him to be more cooperative, rather than having a fight each time you want to load him up and go somewhere. If he tends to back off, and throw his head around, he may well have had a bad experience in the past which he still remembers. If he is young, he may just be nervous. Both types need coaxing, although this needs to be combined with a degree of firmness, since if he once learns his own strength, he will never forget to take advantage of it.

Start off by leading him forward toward the ramp of the trailer, with a bridle on to give you more control. Make sure that the trailer itself is parked on level ground, with chocks beneath the ramp if necessary to prevent it from wobbling when weight is placed on it. The more solid it looks and feels, the more confident he is likely to be about going in. Put the stands down if there are any, leave the towing vehicle in gear, and engage the trailer handbrake. If possible, park it alongside a wall or fence so that there is one less obvious escape route. The interior should be bedded down with straw to give both firm footing and to dampen the noise a little—rubber grip matting will help to do the same. A haynet can be tied up securely and in full view, and the central partition (if there is one) can be moved across to make more room.

Walk forward toward the ramp, remaining between the pony's eye and shoulder; if you try and drag him along, then he is more likely to pull back in resistance than to give in and follow. If he hesitates, offer a tempting feed in a bucket, and try enticing him in. If he does go in, then the feed can be offered as a reward, so that he comes to associate being loaded as a pleasurable event.

If he still proves obstinate, and is not likely to kick out, you could get your assistant to try moving his feet one by one up the ramp. Alternatively a longe rein can be fastened to one side of the trailer, looped around the quarters above the hocks, and pulled taut at the opposite side by your assistant, who should wear gloves so that his/her hands do not become sore. Some horses will

Fig. 44. Holding a longe rein around the quarters of a pony, with the trailer parked against a wall.

immediately give in when they feel something pushing around their quarters, while others may need a good tug on the longe rein before walking in. Should he begin to panic, and reverse rapidly, try and kick out, or rear, you should stop at once, as he is more likely to injure himself than go in. You may have to resort to the more lengthy process of bribing him with treats again.

Sometimes thirst will overcome any fears; leave him without water for 12 hours and then offer him a bucket of water. Allow a short drink if he walks in as a reward.

Some horses and ponies are just naughty about loading, and in such cases, a quick reminder is all that is needed. The easiest approach is to have your assistant hold a yard broom behind the quarters, and to give him a couple of shoves with it. This makes him uncomfortable enough to think twice about digging his heels in, and he will be unable to kick out at the assistant due to the length of the broom handle. Once in, fasten the butt bar, reward with a treat and plenty of praise, and repeat the procedure several times each day until he walks in without any hesitation. If you feed him each day while he is loaded, he will soon come to look forward to going in. Once he has started to behave better, you may want to take him on some short trips. Since there is often a reason for being bad about loading, make sure that it is not due to being given a bad ride by the driver. With time and patience he should get better—but however awkward he may be, do not be tempted to try and ride him in, as this could be extremely dangerous should he try and rear with you on top.

Q. I am moving shortly, and will be transporting my horse to my new home, which is about 300 miles away. Should I stop for a break on the way? If so, should I get my horse out and allow him to stretch his legs?

A. Use your common sense. The types of roads you will be traveling along will make a difference as to the amount of time the journey takes, and the degree of stress it will place on the horse. Highways make for more comfortable and direct driving than twisty, winding roads. Stop every two hours and check on your horse to make sure that he is comfortable, and to offer him a drink of water. He can have a haynet to nibble at, but avoid giving him pellets while in transit. If you really have to, then divide his normal ration into smaller portions which can be fed little and often, otherwise travel colic can arise. Make sure that there is plenty of bedding on the floor; although rubber matting provides a good grip, and seems to absorb a certain amount of vibration, your horse may be reluctant to urinate without a proper bed. Keep an eye on him and see how he is coping with the journey; should he not urinate, and appear uncomfortable because of this, you could break the journey somewhere suitable and unload him so that he has the opportunity to relieve himself.

Q. I am about to buy a trailer, but have never actually towed one before. Are there any tips which would help me?

A. If you are unused to towing, here are some hints. If you are to give your horse a comfortable ride, everything must be in comparatively slow motion. Before loading him up for the first time, you would be well advised to practice driving with the trailer empty until you are accustomed to it—practice on the roads, and work at learning to maneuver it competently in a large field. To assist you when maneuvering, you will find it helpful to have proper side mirrors—if those on your towing vehicle are inadequate or missing, you can purchase these from an auto parts store. Adjust them so that you can see both the trailer mudguards and the road behind you.

Only once you feel confident in your abilities should you risk taking your horse out as a passenger—bad driving will quickly turn him into a poor traveler or bad loader. Anticipate hazards well in advance—avoid driving over potholes, and choose good roads when possible, even if it will take a little longer to reach your destination than a short cut over badly maintained, hilly, or winding roads. Start braking earlier at intersections, and take corners slower and slightly wider, giving plenty of room to any vehicles you overtake. Make sure that the trailer is quite safe before setting off anywhere. The tires should be identical (i.e., bias-ply or radial, not a mixture on the same axle) with a minimum ¼-inch tread depth and with the correct pressure. The lights should all function properly, any required reflectors all present and in place, and the appropriate license plate installed. Make sure that when hitched up the trailer rides level, or very slightly nose downward. If it points upward it may cause snaking, while if it points downward excessively the steering will be less responsive.

Q. How often should I have my trailer serviced?

A. You should have it serviced every six months; the brakes and all moving parts must be checked, and the trailer hitch may also need some attention as they have to undergo quite a lot of stress. Get this done by someone who knows what they are doing, though—an incompetent job could mean a risk to you and your horse.

Q. I am going to buy a trailer shortly, but am unsure as to what kind would be best.

A. This depends upon the size of the animal(s) you wish to tow, and the type of vehicle you intend to tow with. Do not tow up to the legal maximum weight limit, but instead allow yourself to be guided by the recommended trailer towing weights. Each manufacturer publishes a weight, taking into account the size of the engine, the car's overall length, weight, engine size, and suspension, and you should follow these. Otherwise, by attempting to tow too much, you could not only be liable to prosecution if your load is considered unsafe, but it will be difficult to control in bad or emergency conditions if the towing vehicle is not powerful and heavy enough. Most manufacturers or dealers will be only too happy to discuss your requirements, and to suggest a suitable trailer for your purposes.

Q. I am thinking of buying a secondhand trailer; what sort of things should I look out for?

A. There are quite a few checks which should be carried out for condition, safety, and roadworthiness. The floor must be sound, not rotted, and the chassis in good condition. The shock absorbers ought to be properly working on the hitch, the brakes and lights working, and so forth. As when buying a secondhand car, it is best if you can take someone with you who is at least somewhat mechanically minded, and knows a little about trailers.

13
Riding Schools and Training

Q. I would like to learn how to ride, but am rather nervous, and not sure how to go about finding a good riding school. I am worried that I might also be too old to learn.

A. Being nervous is nothing to be ashamed of; what is important is that you find a school where you feel relaxed and at ease, so that any fears you may have will be put to rest. Personal recommendations are best, but if you do not have any friends who ride, look in the Yellow Pages to find out where your local riding schools are, and go and have a look around before you book a lesson. When you arrive, take in your surroundings; they needn't be palatial, but they should at least be clean and tidy. The horses should all look healthy and happy, and any staff should also be tidy and professional, and add an air of efficiency to the place.

Go over to the office and introduce yourself, explaining that you are interested in learning to ride; ask if they have any suitable classes for beginners, and when they are held. To start with, they will probably recommend that you have a few lessons on your own, so that you have some basic control before joining other riders. The attitude of the staff and instructors should be cheerful, friendly, and informative (try and watch a lesson if possible). If

Fig. 45. A group lesson.

you feel that this barn is not quite your scene, do not be put off; try another. For your first lessons, wear a sensible pair of trousers which are not too tight, plus some reasonably flat shoes. The sole should be smooth, not ridged, with a small, well-defined heel (i.e., not sandals or sneakers). The riding school should be able to lend you a hat for your first few lessons; then if you decide that you are enjoying the sport, you could buy your own, plus some jodhpurs and riding boots. As far as age is concerned, you should not worry—provided you take things steadily and are in reasonably good health, you should derive as much enjoyment as someone far younger, although you may find yourself perhaps feeling a little stiffer!

Q. I'd like to rent a horse or a pony so that I can go out for rides with my friend and her horse. Would a riding school do this?

A. It is highly unlikely that a riding school would allow you to rent a horse or pony without supervision from one of their staff. However, a public stable that is in the business of renting horses for pleasure rides, in addition to teaching people how to ride. Some of these stables even administer tests to prospective riders; when you've demonstrated that you can ride to their satisfaction, you will be allowed to rent one of their horses.

Q. I'd like to specialize more in dressage; the riding school I ride at seems to be geared toward jumping all the time. How can I go about learning more?

A. Have a chat with your instructor. If you are in a group lesson, most people usually want to jump rather than concentrate solely on flatwork, so it is often a case of doing a little of everything in order to try and keep the majority happy. Unfortunately, this means that you are unable to progress quite as quickly toward your own particular goal. You might find that the occasional private lesson would be of benefit to you, since although it will cost more, the instruction is more concentrated and the lesson can be structured around doing the things you are especially interested in. Alternatively, ask if there is a different group you can join, which does less jumping. Explain your ambitions; most instructors are only too happy to accommodate, but they are not mind readers and will not know unless you tell them. Should this prove impossible to manage, then you could always change to a different riding school.

Q. I'm not very good at riding, and I'd like to get more experience. I'd also like to learn more about stable management, so that I can one day get my own pony. How can accomplish this?

A. Looking after your own pony can be pretty hard work, so it is important that before buying one, you find out whether you have sufficient knowledge and whether you would enjoy the day-to-day routine of looking after it. Getting wet, muddy, cold, and tired can often make you reconsider!

One of the best ways to find out, and also to generally increase your knowledge, is to ask at local riding schools if it would be possible to help out on weekends and holidays. Some riding schools will give you an occasional lesson, or a small amount of pocket money for your hard work. (This would give you a chance to improve your riding, and also to learn more about caring for a pony.) But as this is not always the rule, don't expect it as your due. They will not necessarily be falling over themselves to get your assistance, since an inexperienced helper can often create extra work for the staff. So be prepared to meet with a few negative responses. If you do succeed in becoming a weekend helper, you will have to be prepared to pull your weight if you want to stay.

Q. I'd like to try and get a summer job at a riding stable, dude ranch, or riding resort—how should I go about it?

A. At first this seems like a great way of getting a free vacation, but it is far less likely to work out that way. Working at a riding resort can be hard, and does not mean that you are going to be included in the guests' social activities as a matter of course. Add to this the fact that many resorts nowadays are also riding schools all year-round, with their own qualified staff, and you will soon see that they are unlikely to welcome you with open arms, especially if you lack experience.

Fig. 46. Resort riding.

However, if you would like to try, are sixteen or over and fairly competent, it might be worth asking, particularly at the smaller stables. Write down all the details of your experience looking after horses and ponies, your standard of riding (be honest about it), and any other points which you feel are in your favor. Be prepared for rejections, and don't expect more than your keep in return for help, with very possibly a small amount of pocket money.

Q. I would like to set up a riding school when I leave school; are there any special qualifications necessary to do this?

A. You don't need qualifications as such if you are sufficiently experienced, but they can be very useful when it comes to attracting clients. To run a school successfully, you will need the experience of a commercial establishment, so it might be worthwhile to become a working student; as such, you barter your time and labor in exchange for lessons, and a stall for your horse. As a working student, you will see more of the day to day running of a stable; and so this would be of more practical benefit to you. You will need to be as businesslike as possible. It would be sensible to take a short computer course, and to learn about bookkeeping and other aspects of running your own business. You might find a part-time or evening course running in your area if you make inquiries. If you prefer, some colleges offer business and equine management courses, but the drawback is that you do spend less time actually working with horses. The more experience you can gain, the better; you may find it helpful to work at a small farm for someone else so that you learn as much as possible about all the ins and outs of it.

Q. I am interested in a career of some kind with horses when I leave school, but am not sure whether I actually want to work with them, and if so in what capacity, or whether to settle for some related job. Are there any addresses I can write to which can send me information on what is involved in various lines of work, and what sort of training is needed?

A. Working with horses involves long and antisocial hours of work, and is often badly paid in comparison to many other jobs; nevertheless, if you are sufficiently dedicated, you may still find it very rewarding work. The best way of finding out whether you would be suited for such a life would be to offer to help out at a local stable for a few weeks. Basic requirements of horses and ponies are the same regardless of the job they do, and it would give you a better idea as to what you were getting yourself into. Should you feel that working in a stable is not for you, but wish to take up some related occupation, there are still plenty of other options open, depending upon where your talents lie, and addresses you can write to for further information are listed in chapter 16.

Q. I am interested in training for a career with horses, and wonder whether there is any form of financial aid available?

A. Financial aid is limited, but some breed and discipline organizations (e.g., the American Quarter Horse Association) offer scholarships for interested students.

You might also consider working at a stable on a working-student basis if you are thinking of taking up teaching as a career, where you will receive instruction in return for providing labor. Any farm that you think may be suitable should always be visited first, of course, taking note of the appearance, condition of the horses, and standard of instruction. You should ask about what you can expect to receive in tuition, your duties and hours of work, time off, and so forth, and who will normally be teaching you. If possible, do have a chat with one or two of the working students already there so that you get a better idea of exactly what goes on.

14

Riding and Road Safety

Q. I need a new riding hat, but there seem to be so many available. I can't afford very much, so would a secondhand one be all right?

A. Never begrudge spending money on sound head protection—lack of it could cost you your life. Probably the best protection is offered by an ASTM-approved safety helmet with a buckled chin strap. All junior (18 and under) horse show riders must, and adults should, wear these helmets.

If you prefer the more traditional velvet- or velveteen-covered riding caps, do not let vanity override safety—always wear it with the chin strap fastened. Whatever hat you choose, it must fit correctly. Different makes often have differently shaped crowns, so it is worth trying several on in the shop to find the best fit. This should be snug, although not so tight that it gives you a headache, and should sit squarely on your head rather than perched on the back like a fashion accessory, as is so frequently seen. If a drawstring is fitted into the liner, it should be tightened up a little so that there is an enclosed pocket of air between the hat and the top of the head, which in the event of a fall would provide a "cushion." Never buy an old hat; always invest in a new one that conforms to the latest ASTM safety standards.

Q. Not long ago my horse was hit by a car. He has now recovered, and is quite sound, but has become very nervous in traffic. Is there anything that can be done to restore his confidence?

A. Horses and ponies have very good memories, and take a long time to forget unpleasant experiences. Although your horse may improve in time, there is no real guarantee. Grazing him in a field near heavy traffic sometimes helps to overcome nervousness, but then there is the risk of being near a major road should he escape, and the fact that actually riding in traffic is quite different. Try to avoid really congested areas, and never ride alone until you are confident in him again. You should still take the precaution of telling someone exactly where you intend to go, and how long you will be, before going out. You will find that the presence of another steady horse will help to give him a bit more confidence; where roads are broad enough and visibility ahead clear, you could keep this horse on your left-hand side. Riding side by side like this will act as a barrier between you and the traffic, and enable you to keep both hands on the reins while your friend gives hand signals. It will encourage drivers to slow down and give you plenty of room when passing, too. (If it is necessary to ride single file, always have the steadier horse in front.)

If you are really worried about the situation and it looks as if your horse may become a real hazard on the roads both to yourself and to other people, then you may have to consider selling him, or else confining your activities to what can be done at home.

Q. Do I always have to ride along the right-hand side of the road? Sometimes I feel my horse would be better off if he faced the traffic passing immediately by him, rather than having his back turned to it.

A. You must always ride on the right side of the road, moving in the same direction that traffic goes. You must obey the rules of the road in the same way as other road users do, stopping for red lights, and so forth.

Q. Which is the correct side to lead a horse from if riding and leading?

A. If you have to ride and lead (which is never a good idea unless both animals are good in traffic, quiet with each other, and you have no other choice), then you should be on the left side, with the horse that's being led on your right. Put a bridle on, so that you have better control, and lead either by the reins, or by looping a lead rein through the bit rings. Keep the led horse's head up by your knee, and try to keep him well in to the side of the road, but with due regard for any pedestrians.

Q. Is it all right to ride along the shoulder?

A. In some areas, grass shoulders seem to be almost the only places where it is possible to have a canter, or give the horse's legs a break from hard road surfaces. However, cantering along them is not very safe, since they often conceal hidden dangers such as soda cans, broken bottles, or drainage ditches. Added to this, should the horse shy at something, he will inevitably move sideways into the path of the traffic; you may not be expecting him to do this, and will therefore be in a bad position to try and prevent it. Some counties do in fact ban horses from being ridden along shoulders, so it is wise to check on this before doing so.

Q. My horse keeps shying at things on shoulders, and at drain covers. How can I stop him, as I am sure that a car will hit him one day when he is doing this?

A. Some horses are very suspicious of anything which looks a bit odd. If your horse has walked over a drain cover before, then the noise and sudden unexpected change in footing may have upset him. Nevertheless, you should get his eyesight checked by the vet, as poor vision could very well account for this habit.

Change your manner of tackling the problem too. Rather than using your right rein when you feel him beginning to spook, use your left leg and left rein to encourage him to bend away from the object. This will control his left shoulder and hindquarters, preventing him from swinging them into the middle of the road in an attempt to keep as far away as possible from whatever it is that frightens him. Apply a similar principle when you hear a truck or noisy vehicle approaching which might alarm him, as it will keep him close to the curb, and likely to move closer toward it rather than into the path of the passing vehicle. He will also be able to see the vehicle as it approaches, out of his left eye; if he is on a right bend instead he is likely to resist your attempts to straighten him, and try to keep his right eye on the vehicle by swinging his quarters toward the center of the road.

Q. Which side of the road should I walk on when leading my horse along the road?

A. You should lead him on the right-hand side of the road, with you on the horse's near (left) side so that you remain between him and any traffic. It is best to use a bridle for better control. Take the reins over his head to lead him, unless he is wearing a running martingale. In that case, either undo the martingale and lead him as described, or keep the reins around his neck but hold them about four inches below the jaw.

Q. Although I don't actually ride in the dark, it is often getting a bit hard to see in the evening when I return home from a ride; I worry in case a driver should fail to see us.

A. There are a number of products which can be used to make yourself more visible. Although fluorescent vests are useful during the daytime, make sure that you buy one with reflective material that will return light when it shines on it. You could also put reflective tape on the back of your saddle, and an armband on your left arm. When leading at night, take the same precautions, and carry in your left hand a flashlight that shines white light to the front, and red light to the back.

15

Hunting

Q. I've never been hunting before, but I would quite like to now that I have my own horse. How do I find out which is my local hunt? And do I have to be a member of it in order to hunt? If so, is it likely to be very expensive?

A. The weekly magazine *The Chronicle of the Horse* is foxhunting's magazine of record, and the Web site of the Masters of Foxhounds Association of America (www.mfha.com) is also an excellent resource. You can find out more about local hunting opportunities by inquiring at riding or boarding stables, or by asking your local riding or Pony Club. Once you have found out which hunt is closest to you, contact its secretary if you wish to join. It varies from one area to another as to whether you have to be a member in order to hunt—some hunts insist that you are a member unless you have been invited as a guest, while others are more relaxed about it and don't mind casual visitors. Your hunt secretary will be able to tell you more about this.

Hunting *is* an expensive sport. In order to become a member you will be required to pay a yearly membership fee, which is used to care for the hounds and to pay for hunt-related expenses. If you are a visitor rather than a member, you will pay a "capping fee" for the privilege of hunting that day (so called because the money is deposited into the hunt secretary's outstretched cap). This amount varies from hunt to hunt.

Q. I hope to go hunting soon—what should I wear? And will I have to carry a hunting whip? My horse is terrified of even a short crop, so I don't know what she would do if I have to carry one.

A. During the cubbing season (when young hounds are introduced to the pack), less formal attire, called "ratcatcher," is allowed. This usually refers to a dark sport coat or riding jacket and a shirt and tie or turtleneck shirt. Some hunts even permit blue jeans or chaps.

For the formal hunting season, hunt staff members wear their livery (usually red coats with white breeches and black boots with tan leather tops). Members who follow as the Field generally wear black coats, buff breeches, and black boots. The stock (hunting tie) is worn with a gold safety pin. Members of the hunt, if granted their colors, will wear red coats. Children may wear a Pony Club or plain-colored tie, jodhpurs, and jodhpur boots. The trend nowadays is more and more towards practicality, and since greater protection is offered by a safety helmet, one of these may be worn if preferred, with a black silk or one of the velvet coverings which are now available.

A hunting whip is always an asset—very practical for opening and shutting gates—but they are expensive and a short crop is quite acceptable. Since your horse has a phobia about whips anyway, you would probably do better to manage without one at all. The most important point about your dress is to ensure that even if you only own a riding jacket, your turnout is tidy and presentable; it is well worth the effort of braiding your horse up, and most

Fig. 47. A hunt meeting.

hunts aren't too fussy provided you make an attempt to arrive with both yourself and your horse looking well groomed. If you are in any doubt whatsoever about the suitability of your dress, contact the hunt secretary.

Q. How many times a week do hounds meet, and how can I find out where?

A. Depending upon the area and numbers, hunts may meet anywhere from two to five days a week. Dates are often advertised in the local press or in *The Chronicle of the Horse*. In some areas hunt

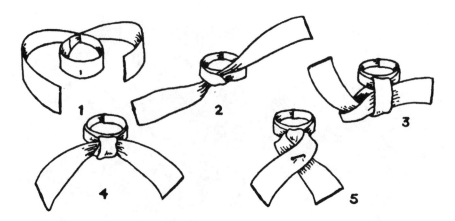

Fig. 48. Stages in the tying of a hunting tie.

saboteurs are active, so in these instances, dates and locations are often passed around by word of mouth, rather than published, but any hunt member or the hunt secretary will be able to tell you.

Q. I am going hunting for the first time, but I am not sure what I should do upon arrival. I have read that I am supposed to greet the Master—are there any others I should make a point of meeting?

A. Courtesy and tradition say that you should first of all greet the Master and wish him a good morning; but bearing in mind that you may not know who he is, or if there is a very large field with many people present, it is understood that this isn't always practical. More importantly, ensure that your horse always stands facing the hounds—never allow him to turn his quarters towards them. If your horse kicks one, you might get sent home in disgrace before you have even started, and you definitely won't be popular!

The secretary or whoever is collecting the capping fees will usually notice you upon arriving, but otherwise you should seek them out and pay them. On seeing any hunt officials, it is of course, only polite to say "good morning." Always follow the Field Master and his instructions; if you need to find a gap in a hedge, or a gateway, be sure to follow the rules of the countryside and avoid damaging crops or disturbing livestock. Remember that the hunt relies upon the goodwill of local landowners to allow them to continue meeting and hunting upon their land.

Q. I am unsure as to whether my tack is suitable for my horse when I take him hunting for the first time. I normally use an All-Purpose saddle, jointed snaffle, and running martingale. Do I need a proper hunting saddle? And should I put boots or bandages on him? I feel that I ought to protect his legs if possible.

A. Your normal tack is fine, provided that it is safe and suitable for jumping and galloping in. Make a point of always checking it very carefully before hunting, for any weak points or rotting stitching. Places where leather comes into contact with metal are always vulnerable to wear and tear, so these points should be thoroughly inspected. If your horse tends to become very strong when in the company of others, use a stronger bit; he will have other horses galloping both in front and beside him, which can prove very exciting for some animals, and it is essential to have good brakes. It is best not to use leg wraps or bandages, as it is likely that you will be encountering some very wet and muddy terrain; after several hours with wet mud working its way between boots and skin your horse will become very uncomfortable. Bandages will quickly become wet and sodden, too. When riding in a cross-country competition, leg protection is quite sensible, but it is then worn for minutes rather than hours, and hunting is rather different.

Q. I don't own a horse, and the local stables won't rent any out. However, my friend and I would like to follow the hunt on foot if we can't do it any other way—are we likely to be told to go away?

A. Lots of people gain a tremendous amount of pleasure and enjoyment from following on foot, in a car, or on horseback—some hunts have a huge following of these "hilltoppers," who want to follow the hunt, but not as members of the Field; they follow in their cars, or if on horseback, they walk or trot to strategic viewing spots. This is a good way to introduce young horses to the hunt.

Q. My friend is taking me hunting with her shortly; I know a little bit but not a great deal. I will be joining her at the meet—are there any special tips I should know about? I don't want to end up committing some terrible sin and embarrassing her!

A. Be careful not to park your trailer or truck at the meet itself, but a reasonable distance away, otherwise problems can arise. If you are away for several hours, perhaps blocking someone in, they can't get out until you return. Also, the area may become very congested with traffic. Try and find somewhere unobtrusive—not right in the middle of some poor farmer's gateway, either. You might find that it is best to transport your horse already saddled up—it will save time, and if your horse becomes excited when he hears the noise, then it will also save you a lot of fuss.

Another tip to remember is that you should consider the fitness of your horse. It can be a very long day, one minute galloping, sometimes for quite long distances, the next standing around in the cold. It requires considerable stamina, and will tire even a fairly fit horse more than you might realize. Your adrenaline will not keep your horse going. Turn for home when he begins to tire, as a weary horse is much more likely to make mistakes or to injure himself—better to save him and enjoy another day's hunting on him in the future.

Q. The last time I went hunting with the Pony Club, my pony was fine while we were standing still, but every time we moved off he got really strong, and was difficult to hold. His last owner hunted him a couple of times and didn't have any trouble stopping him. Should I persevere with a snaffle, which I normally ride in, or change to a pelham? And should I use two pairs of reins with it if I do?

A. When a horse or pony has been hunted a few times, it begins to anticipate what is going to happen and, not surprisingly, will often get excited. It sounds as though this is what has happened with your pony, coupled with the fact that perhaps his previous owner was a bit stronger than you. A change to a pelham when he is hunting sounds like a good idea, so that he has a little more respect for you. Two pairs of reins are more correct on a pelham, so that you can achieve either a snaffle- or a curb-type action on his mouth and head, but if you find it all a bit of a handful to manage, it would be best to use one pair of reins attached to pelham roundings. Check the roundings carefully for safety, as they have to put up with a lot of wear, and are only made of leather.

Q. I'd like to take my horse hunting as I feel it would be good experience for him, but I'm not sure that I like the idea of a fox possibly getting killed at the end of it. Is there an alternative?

A. Though a real fox is rarely chased and killed in the U.S. these days, a more commonly held event here is drag hunting, which is similar to proper hunting in that hounds and hunt staff are present, but instead of chasing a fox, hounds follow an artificial scent which has previously been laid over a specially prepared line of country. It can be quite exciting as you are guaranteed a fast run with plenty of fences to jump.

Q. Are there any special things I should do for my horse when he comes back from hunting?

A. The care of a horse after hunting (or indeed, a cross-country event) is just as important as the preparation beforehand. Once you return home, check him over very carefully for any cuts, scrapes, or thorns which may have become embedded in the legs. You can find the latter by running your fingers gently upward against the lie of the hair; should you find a thorn, trim the hair away from the area, withdraw it with a pair of tweezers, and poultice. All cuts, however trivial they may seem, should be dealt with promptly, since neglecting them could allow an infection to build up which will put the horse out of work for some time. Check also for over-reaches—cuts in the heels of the front feet—since these are sometimes concealed by a flap of skin. It is best not to wash off muddy legs unless treatment for an injury is required, but rather to let them dry naturally, after which the mud can be brushed off. Washing tends to work dirt into the pores of the skin, which often remain open for some time when the horse is tired, and this could set up a nasty infection.

If the horse is to remain stabled for the night, then put a set of stable bandages on which will help to support tired legs and ensure that he is warm enough (a tired horse is less able to create as much body heat). Remove the worst of the mud and sweat, but don't make too much of a fuss—just do enough to make him comfortable for the night. Put yourself in the same position; after a strenuous day, quite often all you feel like doing is sitting down and putting your feet up with a bit of peace and quiet.

Rather than giving him his normal feed, give a bran mash instead which will have a laxative effect and ensure that his digestive system does not seize up through tiredness. Add a double handful of glucose to it as well as Epsom salts, as this will make it both more palatable, and help perk him up a bit so that he feels the effects of tiredness less. If he is to be turned out for the night, make sure that he is dry first, as a wet coat in cold weather will lead to him getting chilled. If he is able to stay in, put an anti-sweat sheet on beneath his normal blankets in case he starts sweating again during the evening. This sometimes happens if the horse has an excitable nature, or if he is very tired and the skin pores take a long time to start functioning properly again. You should check him later in the evening to make sure that he is comfortable and there are no further problems. The next day, he will probably appreciate a day off, and should be either turned out, led out in hand, or ridden out in walk for half an hour so that he has a chance to stretch his legs and loosen up any stiffness.

16

What to Join and Useful Addresses

For information on particular equine breeds and equestrian activities, contact the following associations and organizations:

Breed Organizations

American Bashkir Curly Registry
P.O. Box 246, Ely, Nevada 89301-0246
(775) 289-4999, fax: (775) 289-8579
www.abcregistry.org

American Connemara Pony Society
2360 Hunting Ridge Rd., Winchester VA 22603
(540) 662-5953, fax: (540) 722-2277
information@acps.org; www.americanconnemara.org

American Hanoverian Society
4067 Iron Works Parkway, Suite 1, Lexington, Kentucky 40511
(859) 255-4141, fax: (859) 255-8467
ahsoffice@aol.com, www.hanoverian.org

American Holsteiner Horse Association, Inc.
222 East Main St., #2, Georgetown, KY 40324-1712
(502) 863-4239, fax (502) 868-0722
holsteiner@igc.org, www.holsteiner.com

American Indian Horse Registry, Inc.
9028 State Park Rd., Lockhart, TX 78644-9713
(512) 398-6642
www.indianhorse.com

American Morgan Horse Association
122 Bostwick Rd., Shelburne, VT 05482
(802) 985-4944, fax: (802) 985-8897
info@morganhorse.com, www.morganhorse.com

American Mustang and Burro Association, Inc.
P.O. Box 788, Lincoln, CA 95648
(530) 633-9271, fax: (916) 632-1855
ambainc@bardalisa.com, www.bardalisa.com

American Paint Horse Association
P.O. Box 961023, Fort Worth, Texas 76161-0023
(817) 834-APHA (2742), fax: (817) 834-3152
askapha@apha.com, www.apha.com

American Quarter Horse Association
P.O. Box 200, Amarillo, TX 79168-0001
(806) 376-4811, fax: (806) 349-6401
www.aqha.com, e-mail can be sent through Web site

American Saddlebred Horse Association
4093 Iron Works Pkwy, Lexington, KY 40511
(859) 259-2742, fax: (859) 259-1628
saddlebred@asha.net, www.saddlebred.com

American Shire Horse Association
P.O. Box 739, New Castle, CO 81647
(970) 876-5980, fax: (970) 876-1977
secretary@shirehorse.org, www.shirehorse.org

American Sportpony Division (Affiliated with American Warmblood Registry)
P.O. Box 1236, Jackson, CA 95642

(209) 245-3565, fax: (530) 756-0892
awr@davis.com, www.americansportpony.com

American Trakehner Association
1520 West Church St., Newark, OH 43055
(740) 344-1111, fax: (740) 344-3225
atahorses@alltel.net, www.americantrakehner.com

American Warmblood Society
2 Buffalo Run Rd., Center Ridge, AR 72027
(501) 893-2777, fax: (501) 893-2779
aws@americanwarmblood.org, www.americanwarmblood.org

Appaloosa Horse Club
2720 W. Pullman Rd., Moscow, ID 83843
(208) 882-5578, fax: (208) 882-8150
aphc@appaloosa.com, www.appaloosa.com

Appaloosa Sport Horse Association
3380 Saxonburg Blvd., Glenshaw, PA 15116
(412) 767-4616
apsha@netrax.net, www.netrax.net/aliasme/

Arabian Sport Horse Association, Inc.
6145 Whaleyville Blvd., Suffolk, VA 23438-9730
(757) 986-4486
ppleban@odu.edu, www.arab-sporthorse.com

Belgian Warmblood Breeding Association/North American District
136 Red Fox Trail, Chapin, SC 29036
(304) 728-6140, fax: (304) 725-1924
nabwp@aol.com, www.belgianwarmblood.com

Cleveland Bay Horse Society of North America
P.O. Box 483, Goshen, NH 03752
Phone/fax: (603) 863-5193
janeescott@yahoo.com, www.c-zone.net/wheelgat/cb1.html

Friesian Horse Association of North America
P.O. Box 11217, Lexington, KY 40574-1217
Phone: (541) 549-4272, fax: (541) 549-4770
fhana@psyberia.com, www.fhana.com

Friesian Horse Society, Inc.
1302 South Duncanville Rd., Cedar Hill, TX 75104
(972) 274-0629, fax: (972) 274-0497
fhs@sunlink.net, www.friesianhorsesociety.com

Haflinger Breeders Organization, Inc.
14640 State Route 83, Coshocton, OH 43812-8911
(740) 829-2790, fax: (740) 829-2322
hbo@coshocton.com, www.stallionstation.com/hbo/hbo.html

Hungarian Horse Association of America
HC 71, Box 108, Anselmo, NE 68813
(308) 749-2411, fax (308) 749-2413
hhaa@horseplaza.com, www.horseplaza.com/breeds.htm

International Andalusian & Lusitano Horse Association
101 Carnoustie North, #200, Birmingham, AL 35242
(205) 995-8900, fax: (205) 995-8966
office@ialha.com, www.ialha.com

International Arabian Horse Association
10805 E. Bethany Dr., Aurora, CO 80014-2605
(303) 696-4500, fax: (303) 696-4599
iaha@iaha.com, www.iaha.com

International Buckskin Horse Association
P.O. Box 268, Shelby, IN 46377-0268
Phone/fax: (219) 552-1013
ibha@netnitco.net, www.ibha.org

International Sporthorse Registry/Oldenburg N.A.
939 Merchandise Mart, Chicago, IL 60654-1102
(312) 527-6544, fax: (312) 527-6573
isreg@aol.com, www.isroldenburg.org

Irish Draught Horse Society of North America
5480 Major Lane, Platteville, WI 53818
(608) 348-2519
info@irishdraught.com, www.irishdraught.com

Lipizzan Association of North America
P.O. Box 1133, Anderson, IN 46015-1133
(765) 644-3904, fax: (765) 644-3361
lana@lipizzan.org, www.lipizzan.org

National Show Horse Registry, Inc.
10368 Bluegrass Pkwy., Louisville, KY 40299
(502) 266-5100, fax (502) 266-5806
nshowhorse@aol.com, www.nshregistry.org

New Forest Pony Association & Registry
Log Cabin Farm, 362 Wakefield Rd., Pascoag, RI 02859
(401) 568-8238, fax (401) 567-0311
lugil@earthlink.net, www.newforestpony.net

North American Selle Français Association, Inc.
P.O. Box 604, Round Hill, Virginia 20142
(540) 338-0166, fax: (540) 338-0169
sellefrancais@starpower.net, www.sellefrancais.org

Norwegian Fjord Horse Registry
1203 Appian Dr., Webster, NY 14580
(716) 872-4114, fax: (716) 787-0497
registrar@nfhr.com, www.nfhr.com

Oldenburg Horse Breeders Society
150 Hammocks Drive
West Palm Beach, FL 33413-2054
(561) 969-0709, fax: (561) 969-0064
oldenburg@flinet.com, www.oldenburghorse.com

Palomino Horse Breeders of America
15253 E. Skelly Dr., Tulsa, OK 74116-2637

(918) 438-1234, fax: (918) 438-1232
yellahrses@aol.com, www.palominohba.com

Performance Horse Registry, Inc.
4047 Iron Works Parkway, Lexington, KY 40511
(859) 258-2472, fax: (859) 231-6662
phr@equestrian.org, www.equestrian.org/phr/

Pinto Horse Association of America, Inc.
1900 Samuels Ave., Ft. Worth, TX 76102-1141
(817) 336-7842, fax: (817) 336-7416
registration@pinto.org, www.pinto.org

Pony of the Americas Club, Inc.
5240 Elmwood Ave., Indianapolis, IN 46203
(317) 788-0107, fax: (317) 788-8974
poac@iquest.net, www.poac.org

Swedish Warmblood Association of North America
P.O. Box 788, Socorro, NM 87801
(505) 835-1318, fax: (505) 835-1321
swana@sdc.org, www.swedishwarmblood.org

Thoroughbred Horses for Sport
P.O. Box 160, Great Falls, VA 22066
(703) 759-6273
sporthw@erols.com, www.sporthorseworld.com

United States Lipizzan Registry
707 13th St. SE, Suite 275, Salem, OR 97301
(503) 589-3172, fax: (503) 362-6393
uslroffice@aol.com, www.lipizzan-uslr.com

Welsh Pony and Cob Society of America, Inc.
P.O. Box 2977, Winchester, VA 22604-2977
(540) 667-6195, fax: (540) 667-3766
wpcsa@crosslink.net, www.welshpony.org

Westfalen Horse Association
2820 N. Liberty Rd., NE, North Liberty, IA 52317
(319) 626-2516, fax: 319-626-2493
joandeere@aol.com, www.westfalenhorse.com

Activity organizations

American Buckskin Registry Association
PO Box 3850
Redding, CA 96049
(530) 223-1420
www.americanbuckskin.org

American Competition for Riders with Disabilities
5303 Felter Road
San Jose, CA 95132
(408) 261-8292 phone
(408) 261-9438 fax
http://members.aol.com/ACORDCOMP/

American Donkey & Mule Society
P.O. Box 1210
Lewisville TX 75067
(972) 219-0781 phone
(972) 420-9980 fax
adms@juno.com; www.geocities.com/lovelongears/

American Driving Society
2324 Clark Road
Lapeer, MI 48446
(810) 664-8666
FAX (810) 664-2405
www.americandrivingsociety.org

The American Driving Society
Box 160
Metamora, MI 48455

(810) 664-8666; fax: (810)664-2405 fax
www.americandrivingsociety.org

American Endurance Ride Conference
P.O. Box 6027
Auburn, CA 95604
Phone: 530.823.2260
Fax: 530.823.7805
Email: aerc@foothill.net

American Miniature Horse Association
5601 South Interstate 35 W
Alvarado, TX 76009
(817) 783-5600
www.amha.com; www.minihorses.com

American Morgan Horse Association
PO Box 960
Shelburne, VT 05482
(802) 985-4944; fax: (802)985-8897
www.morganhorse.com

American Paint Horse Association
P.O. Box 961023
Fort Worth, TX 76161-0023
(817) 834-APHA; fax: (817) 834-3152
www.apha.com

American Quarter Horse Association
P.O. Box 200
Amarillo, TX 79168
(806) 376-4811; fax: (806) 349-6401
www.aqha.org
The American Shetland Pony Club—
The American Miniature Horse Registry
81 B Queenwood Road
Morton, IL 61550
(309)263-4044; fax: (309) 263-5113
info@shetlandminiature.com

Appaloosa Horse Club
2720 West Pullman Road
Moscow, ID 83843
(208) 882-5578; fax: (208)882-8150
www.appaloosa.com

Canadian Equestrian Federation
2460 Lancaster Road
Ottawa, Ontario K1B 4S5
(613) 248-3433; fax: (613) 248-3484 fax
www.equinecanada.com

The Chronicle of the Horse
P.O. Box 46
Middleburg, VA 20118
Telephone: (540) 687-6341
Fax: (540) 687-3937
www.chronofhorse.com

Federation Equestre Internationale
Avenue Mon Repos 24
1000 Lausanne 5, Switzerland
41 21 310 47 47; fax: 41 21 310 47 60
www.horsesport.org

Intercollegiate Horse Shows Association
P.O. Box 108
Fairfield, CT 06430
(203)259-5100; fax: (203)256-9377
www.ihsa.com

Masters of Foxhounds Association of America
P.O. Box 363
Millwood, VA 22646
Telephone: (540) 955-5680
Fax: (540) 955-5682
www.mfha.com

National Cutting Horse Association
4704 Highway 377 So
Fort Worth, TX 76116-8805
(817)244-6188; fax:
www.nchacutting.com

National Disability Sports Alliance
25 W. Independence Way,
Kingston, RI 02881
(401) 792-7130; fax: (401) 792-7132
www.ndsaonline.org

National Snaffle Bit Association
4815 S. Sheridan, Suite 109
Tulsa, OK 74145
(918)270-1469; fax: (918)270-1471
www.nsba.com

North American Riding for the Handicapped
P.O. Box 33150
Denver, CO 80233
(800) 369-Ride; fax: (303) 252-4610 fax
www.narha.org

USA Equestrian (USAEq) [formerly American Horse Shows Association]
4047 Iron Works Parkway
Lexington, KY 40511
(859)258-2472; fax: (859)231-6662
www.equestrian.org

United States Dressage Federation
220 Lexington Green Circle, Suite 500
Lexington, KY 40503
(859)971-2277; fax: (859)971-7722
www.www.usdf.org

Index

Stiffness, rider's, 18–19
  exercises for, 22–24
Stirrup bar, 55
Stirrup length, 18–19
  correct, 20–21, **21**
  extending, 16–17, **17**
Stock (hunting tie), 174, **176**
Stone wall fencing, 64, **65**
Straps
  belly, 44, 45, **45,** 55
  crib, 77–78, **78**
  leg, 44, 45
Straw
  eating, 75–76
  and respiratory problems, 126–27
Stubbornness, 21–22
Studs, 108–10, **109**
Sugar beet pulp, 84–85
Sunburned nose, 119
Supplements, vitamin/mineral, 76, 79–80
  for hooves, 114
Surcingle, fit of, 54–55
Swaying. *See* Weaving
Sweat, 79, 80
Sweat clip, 100, **101**

T
Tack
  cleaning, 46–47, 50
  fit of, 13, 28
  for hunting, 177
  secondhand, 51
Tail
  bandages, 151
  pulling, **92,** 92–93, 125
  rubbing, **135,** 135–36
  shampooing, 91
  thinning, 89
Teeth
  estimating age by, 120, **121,** 122–23
  frequency of exams, 5, 136
  missing, 123
  and nipping, 96
  problems, and leaning on hands, 27
  sharp, 43, 119–20
  and weight, 84
Temperament, horse/pony
  high-strung, 77
  importance of, 4–5, 7–8
Temperature, in healthy horse/pony, 137
Thrush, 127
Toy, horse/pony, 72, 84
Trace clip, 100, **101**
Traffic, riding in, 168
Trailer
  kicking while stopped, 153
  loading horse, 153–54, **154**

recommended towing weights, 157–58
  renting, 149
  secondhand, 158
  servicing, 157
  side to transport on, 149
  towing, 156–57
  unloading from, 151–52, **152**
Transporting. *See* Traveling
Traveling, 149–59
  clothes for, **150,** 150–51
  long distances, 155–56
Treats, giving, 69–70
Tree, saddle, 41, 52, **53**
Trigger clip, **75**
Trimming comb. *See also* Clipping, 92–93
Trot, rising, 19–20, **20**
  and stirrup length, 21
Turnout blanket, 44, 50
  caring for, 49
Twitch, **92,** 93, 103
Tying up, 98–99, **99**

U
Udder, washing, 98
Unloading, from trailer, 151–52, **152**
USA Equestrian, 140–41, 194
Use of pony/horse, when leasing, 3

V
Vaccinations, 5, 136
Vaulting on, 145–46, **146**
Veterinary
  bills, 2, 5
  certificate, 5–7
  problems, 119–38
  when to call, 128, 129, 130, 136–38
"Vetting," 6–7
Vulva, washing, 98

W
Water bucket, kicking, 69
Weaving, 73, **74,** 77
Weeds, removing, 59, 62
Weight, of horse/pony, 75, 134
  keeping on, 84–85
Whip
  dressage, 26
  hunting, 174
Whiskers, grooming, 95
Windsucking, 77–78, **78**
  and colic, 88
Winter, expenses in, 5
Withers, and blankets, 54–55
Wood, chewing, 76
Worming, 64, 135
  and colic, 88
  and weight, 84